Gene Basset's Vietnam Sketchbook

Thom Rooke

Gene Basset's Vietnam Sketchbook

A Cartoonist's Wartime Perspective

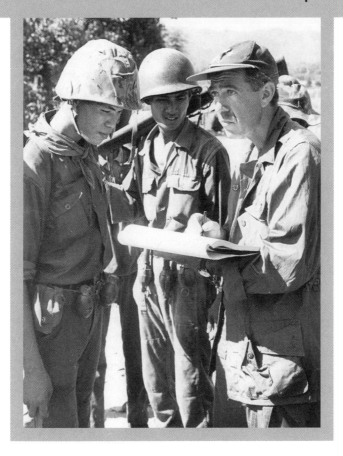

Syracuse University Press

Title page: Gene Basset in Vietnam, 1965.
Photography by Koichi Sawada. Courtesy of Gene Basset.

First Edition 2015

15 16 17 18 19 20   6 5 4 3 2 1

∞ The paper used in this publication meets the minimum requirements
of the American National Standard for Information Sciences—Permanence
of Paper for Printed Library Materials, ANSI Z39.48-1992.

For a listing of books published and distributed by Syracuse University Press,
visit www.SyracuseUniversityPress.syr.edu.

ISBN: 978-0-8156-3421-8 (cloth)   978-0-8156-1057-1 (paperback)
978-0-8156-5337-0 (e-book)

Library of Congress Cataloging-in-Publication Data

Gene Basset's Vietnam sketchbook : a cartoonist's wartime perspective /
Thom Rooke. — First Edition.

pages cm

Includes bibliographical references.

ISBN 978-0-8156-3421-8 (cloth : alk. paper) — ISBN 978-0-8156-1057-1 (pbk.) —
ISBN 978-0-8156-5337-0 (e-book) 1. Basset, Gene, 1927—Notebooks, sketchbooks,
etc. 2. Vietnam War, 1961–1975—Art and the war. I. Rooke, Thom W.,
author. II. Basset, Gene, 1927– Drawings. Selections.

NC1429.B32A4 2015

741.5'69—dc23   2015017970

Manufactured in the United States of America

From the Author

This book is dedicated to

PAUL REVERE

Rock legend,
founder of Paul Revere and the Raiders,
entertainer extraordinaire.

Julie and I cherish our friendship with you and Syd.

Your work with veterans of the Vietnam War,
especially the Ride to the Wall Foundation,
is an inspiration to all.

From the Artist

To the Vietnam old hacks,
photogs, and scribes,
who reported from up front,
my admiration and recognition
for a hell-of-a-job!

Contents

Illustrations

Preface

This book is about the Vietnam War. Although I grew into young adulthood during this era, I somehow managed to miss the war. I wasn't drafted. I didn't fight. I never chained myself to a tree in front of city hall, organized a sit-in in the Dean's office, nor plotted anti-establishment mayhem with dope-smoking hippies. I did not steal the Pentagon Papers, riot on campus, move to Canada, burn the flag, accuse the military-industrial complex of committing a variety of crimes against humanity, or bake cookies for the boys overseas. I never had a friend or family member come home in a body bag. No, it wasn't fair. But by missing the war I was left with a relatively unbiased perspective, one that has allowed me to look back at it—almost half a century later—with a genuine objectiveness that remains impossible for many of my peers.

On the other hand, those who did participate in the Vietnam War, including the dubious types of war-related "participation" just described, typically developed a unique, often subjective, view of the conflict. (I use the word *participated* with appropriate caution—I'm not implying that the fellow who burned his draft card in front of the ROTC building somehow "participated" in the war to the same extent as the guy who took fire in a rice paddy. I'm merely acknowledging that there are different ways to experience a war, and through these experiences one can become an "expert" on certain war-related topics.) Some of these participants went on to write about the war. The entanglement in Vietnam may not have inspired as many literary outpourings as more noble and romantic conflicts like the American Revolution, the Civil War, or World War II, but there have still been enough books and articles written about Vietnam to fill a C-130 Hercules transport plane. Amazon lists about a dozen items in its "Essential Vietnam War Books" section, and the website Goodreads has over 1,000 entries on its site for popular Vietnam

War books.[1] More than seventy-five movies about the Vietnam War have been filmed.[2] Over the past five decades endless pro- and anti-war sentiments have found their way into television commentaries, radio talk-show interviews, newspaper articles, political speeches, classroom lectures, and pretty much every other forum for national debate. It seems that any lesson Vietnam can teach has, in some fashion, already been taught. Some of these lessons must be fairly complex because it's often claimed that the best minds in government have failed—repeatedly—to learn them; others are simple enough to appreciate even when they're written in crayon on a damp piece of cardboard carried by a fatigues-wearing veteran on cold street corners. But whether the messages are complex or simple, they often come attached to strong emotions and biases that can cloud their delivery. If there is anything of value that a person who missed the war—as I did—may be able to bring to this discussion, it's a genuinely objective perspective.

Luckily, not everything about the Vietnam War needs to be analyzed by war experts. Nor is everything controversial. (See *A Layman's Guide* insert.) The events leading up to America's involvement in the conflict are relatively straightforward[3] and only the delusional deny that the consequences of the subsequent war were chilling. Just how bad was it?[4]

- Over 2.5 million Americans served in Vietnam
- Over 1.7 million Americans were drafted for the war
- Almost 60,000 Americans were killed
- Over 300,000 Americans were wounded
- The last man was drafted on June 30, 1973

The final bullet point has personal significance. In June 1973 I was a seventeen-year-old high school student living near Detroit. Every guy my age knew that Nixon had just ended the draft, but I figured I might somehow still get called up. I was nervously awaiting the arrival of a letter from Washington containing the ominous words, "Greetings from the President of the United States . . ." The letter never came. When it was clear that I wouldn't be joining the military I headed off to the University of Michigan and enrolled as a freshman. The class of 1978 was the first entirely "post-draft" class to enter college, and I thus led the first generation of collegians to

A Layman's Guide

EVENTS LEADING TO THE VIETNAM WAR

French colonial rule of Indochina (including the region that would eventually become Vietnam) was established during the 1800s and remained in effect for nearly a century. Despite efforts by China and the United States to contain Japanese expansionism, Japan tossed out the French in 1940–41. The Japanese controlled Indochina until their surrender to the Allies in 1945. In the power vacuum that followed, Ho Chi Minh and his People's Congress declared independence for Vietnam. The French, anxious to regain territory taken from them during their drubbing in the Pacific, quickly committed military forces to oppose this revolution. The Vietnam War was officially "on."

On, perhaps—but at this stage it was largely a war by proxy. By 1950, the United States was aiding the French, while the Russians and Chinese were abetting anyone who opposed the French. It was clear by 1954 that France, having once again achieved its quota of major military defeats for any given war, was in serious trouble. A multinational group convened in Geneva to discuss the situation in Vietnam failed to resolve the key issues driving the conflict; a line was subsequently drawn along the 17th Parallel dividing the country into North-South sides. The French pulled out completely in 1956.

For the ensuing eight years, the Vietnamese forces of the South, quietly egged on by the United States and others, battled the forces of the North who were now fully supported by the Chinese and Russians. In 1964, early into Lyndon Johnson's presidency, an incident occurred in the Gulf of Tonkin in which an American destroyer, the USS *Maddox*, was allegedly attacked by North Vietnamese gunboats. President Johnson was reflexively authorized by Congress to "take all necessary measures . . . to prevent further aggression." With that, the United States officially entered the war.

see the Vietnam War entirely from the safety of hindsight. President Ford finally declared the war "finished" in 1975;[5] I was almost midway through my college career when this milestone occurred. A mere two years later, when I graduated and moved on to medical school, Vietnam had already become a mostly forgotten issue on campus.

How did I end up collaborating on this particular book? The answer requires me to fast-forward about twenty years . . .

I first crossed paths with Gene Basset in 2000. Despite our generational differences, my wife and I became friends with him and his wife,

Ann. Topping the list of things I find fascinating about Gene is his occupation—cartoonist. For those wondering what it takes to make a career in this field, a look at Gene's path illustrates the rigors involved.

We eventually began collaborating on various ventures; these were mostly things I talked him into doing (like writing children's books with me and paying more attention to his health) but occasionally the undertakings came at Gene's suggestion. (For example, he encouraged me to pursue art as a hobby and learn how to drink martinis without getting sick. I failed spectacularly at both.) As I got to know him better, Gene began to show me more of the massive body of work he'd created and stashed away over the previous sixty years. I'm not sure that he ever really intended to have me look at all this stuff, but things kept coming up in conversation ("Illegal pirating of software? Oh yeah . . . I think I did a drawing of that once. Let me look around for it . . .") and he'd eventually produce the goods.

It's hard to think of an idea that Gene hasn't already turned into a cartoon. He would show me things he'd drawn years ago. Then

A Layman's Guide to Gene Basset and the Road to Professional Cartooning

Gene was born July 24, 1927. After realizing at an early age that "it was a lot easier to draw pictures than actually work for a living," Gene embarked upon a career in art. He earned his Bachelor of Arts degree from Brooklyn College and made additional educational stops at the University of Missouri, Cooper Union, Pratt Institute, and the New York Art Students League. As WWII wound down, he served a two-year stint in the Coast Guard before taking his artistic abilities to the private sector. For the next forty years Gene zigzagged through the exclusive world of political cartooning, moving from job to job as opportunities came and went. Early employment gigs included sketch artist at the *Indianapolis Times*, Broadway caricaturist for the *Brooklyn Eagle*, sports cartoonist for the *Boston Post*, and editorial cartoonist for the *Honolulu Star Bulletin*. In 1962 he joined Scripps Howard News Service as chief editorial cartoonist; he also started syndicating his work through United Features. Gene left Scripps Howard and became the editorial cartoonist for the *Atlanta Journal* in 1982 and stayed there until "retiring" in Saint Peter, Minnesota. During this time he also prepared a weekly cartoon on state and local politics for the *Mankato Free Press*.

"HOW UTTERLY EXCITING .. I'VE NEVER MET A SOFTWARE PIRATE."

more things. Five drawings became ten. Ten became a hundred. The more I saw—thousands of cartoons covering politics, sports, theatre, business, agriculture, and a dozen other topics that ought to be too obscure for cartoons—the more impressed I became (even when I was the unwitting subject of his attention).

Somewhere along the way I reached the point where I became so impressed with all the sketches I'd seen that there was no point in Gene showing me any more of his work. It's entirely plausible that we are born with a finite capacity to be impressed with any given subject; if so, I'd apparently reached my limit.

Or so I thought. And then I saw what Gene brought back from the war . . .

One afternoon over cocktails, Gene and I were discussing some obtuse aspect of the United States' ongoing involvement in Iraq—or maybe it was Afghanistan? He started reminding me that the government was "repeating the mistakes of the past." To illustrate his point, Gene hurried off to his basement and returned minutes later with a collection of drawings he had made more than forty years earlier in Vietnam. There were seventy or eighty sketches, each mounted in the same fragile wood-and-plastic lime-green frames they'd been

THE ANATOMY LESSON OF DR. ROOKE. 1632
WITH APOLOGIES TO REMBRANDT VAN RIJN

placed in decades ago when he'd last exhibited them. I slowly flipped through the drawings as he explained their origin.

According to Gene, in 1965 he had attended a social gathering in Washington hosted by his employers du jour, the admittedly conservative Scripps Howard News Service. Also in attendance was Earl Richert, who at that time was head of the news division. One of the topics Gene discussed with his boss that evening was the rapidly escalating war in Vietnam—it was, after all, the hottest sociopolitical issue of the moment and a common subject for political cartoons. In the relaxed party atmosphere, a bargain was struck between Gene and Richert: the Scripps Howard News Service was sending Gene to Vietnam to cover the war. As Gene put it, "We just kind of came up with the idea. This was not just another job—I was genuinely excited at the proposal. I probably shouldn't have been. I'm not sure either one of us thought things through very carefully. We just decided to do it."

It was an assignment perhaps more fitting for a conventional war correspondent than a political cartoonist but, even after everyone sobered up, the idea of Gene going to Vietnam somehow remained viable. More likely, it was one of those situations where nobody—including Gene—wanted to admit that the idea of sending a middle-aged cartoonist to weigh in on a war taking place in Southeast Asia might not be as great as it seemed when the gin first suggested it. But no one blinked or backed down, so Gene put his life "on hold" and prepared to ship off to Vietnam, where he would spend approximately three months performing the task for which he'd been sent. Gene still recalls the disruption to his life created by this trip. "I was working on a movie in Hollywood. They were filming Blake Edwards' *What Did You Do in the War, Daddy?* and I was sketching promotional 'title art' for the project. That's how strange life can be. One day I'm making drawings in a perfect mock-up of a bombed-out World War II Italian village complete with tanks and soldiers, the next day I'm doing the same kind of drawings in a real war."

Looking at them almost fifty years later, Gene's Vietnam War drawings still deliver a powerful impact. When I first saw them I didn't understand why they affected me so strongly. These sketches don't depict the classic "images of war" that have become the staple of magazines, television, and movies. Classic war images, typically captured in cold reality by delicate black boxes with names like Rolleiflex and Leica, tend to be violent and emotionally charged: dying soldiers, mutilated limbs, puddles of blood, faces contorted in anger or agony, suffering civilians, crying orphans. Gene's etchings have none of these elements. They are simple sketches depicting simple, usually peaceful, scenes. Gene claims that he would choose subjects that attracted him, then allow no more than ten or fifteen minutes for a quick drawing. Shading might be added later to create a more "finished" product. The roughness of the sketches did nothing to detract from them—indeed, as pure artwork, they are striking. Gene himself recognized the inherent artistic quality of these drawings, albeit in his own modest fashion. When asked if these drawings were "good art" he replied, "I think so. I can sketch pretty well, but I'll be the first to admit that I'm not a great draftsman. Lots of artists are technically better than me, but my drawings—the spontaneous stuff, at least—were admired by my peers as something they either couldn't do—or didn't do."

I eventually hung some on the walls of my house as decorative art, and the responses from neighbors, guests, and assorted household

Vietnam, 1965

Lyndon Johnson took the oath of office for the presidency of the United States on January 20, 1965; later that year Gene, traveled to Vietnam. The fact that there was still a war for Gene to sketch may have ultimately come as a surprise for Johnson. He quite possibly expected things to be winding down by year's end.

After all, American military might was ramping up rapidly into an unstoppable force that seemed destined to dominate the Communist opposition. America's commitment to ground forces began in March with the introduction of 3,500 marines sent to beef up defenses; they joined a much larger number of "advisors" already in place. The number of combat soldiers would grow to almost 200,000 by the end of the year. The initiation of Rolling Thunder, a program of sustained strategic bombing, promised to demoralize and destroy the enemy. Early battle victories at Chu Lai in August (Operation Starlite) and La Drang in the fall seemed to predict an inevitable U.S. victory. While no military campaign is ever free from setbacks, the situation in 1965 certainly looked promising.

Apparently the rest of the nation had a similar positive vibe. The October 22, 1965, issue of *Time* magazine featured a photo of soldiers being ferried into battle by helicopter and bore the caption "The turning point in Vietnam." A Gallop poll from August 27, 1965, asked if U.S. involvement in Vietnam was a "mistake": only 24 percent of those surveyed thought that it was (that number grew to 61 percent by May 14, 1971).

Johnson, perhaps not inappropriately, expected the North to seek a political solution; in a speech delivered at Johns Hopkins University on April 7, 1965, he offered not only a moral justification for the war but also a high-priced solution involving a billion dollars in aid and support for a Mekong River project to "provide food and water and power on a scale to dwarf even our own TVA . . ." It was, in his mind, a deal the North couldn't refuse.

Except that they did . . .

dignitaries were overwhelmingly positive. I wasn't surprised that my male friends liked the drawings; the men I know are hard-wired to appreciate a good war motif. What surprised me was how much women seemed to like them as well. When I pressed Gene to elaborate on the reasons he thought his drawings were so well received by a broad segment of viewers, he offered that "I think what people like is the humor and the 'magic' of creation. Nobody else had done much with spontaneous drawing like this—at least not in a war setting.

They were done in ink so it was definitely a case of 'first impression.' I couldn't significantly change anything later. People notice [a distinct style like] this."

After my first viewing, I voiced my opinion that Gene ought to publish these drawings—and that I should find a way to help with the project. (I may appear as the "sole author" of this work, but only because Gene has chosen not to include himself as an author. He feels that his role in the production of the book is self-explanatory. Regardless of authorship or titles, this book is a true collaboration, both in work and in spirit.) As I tried to envision how such a publication might be structured, I foresaw a potentially embarrassing problem: I wasn't sure exactly what Gene was trying to say with his sketches. The collection was visually impressive, but as a collective work it wasn't sending me any specific message. I wanted to find something pithy and powerful and important in his pictures, but all I saw were scenes of people trying their best to survive the slow grind of war. What is Gene trying to tell me? These drawings weren't trying to convince me that "war is hell." They didn't depict war as noble, or futile, or morally wrong. Yes, the sketches touched a nerve. Yes, they moved me. It just wasn't clear why.

I needed an answer, so one night over Pinot Noir I asked Gene a few questions that later, under the influence of sobriety, seemed like they may have been a tad too direct: "Gene, what's so important about these drawings? What were you trying to say? What bold statement did you think you were making when you drew them?"

Gene thought for a moment, then shrugged. "Statement? Nothing. I just drew what I saw. I tried not to let things influence me. Of course, you can't sketch something without becoming part of the scene yourself, so I suppose you could always say that I must have been influenced a little by the things going on around me."

Fascinating. The man had spent three months in Vietnam "drawing whatever caught my eye" for newspaper readers back home, and more than forty years later, looking back at the collection en masse, neither of us could figure out precisely what event, lesson, emotion— what anything—Gene was trying to capture with his drawings.

That changed. It was nearly a year before it finally occurred to me that one answer to the riddle of "what is Gene trying to say" could be found by comparing his sketches to the "cold," reality-based photographs mentioned earlier. Photography has been vital to the depiction of war since the work of Matthew Brady in the American Civil War;[6] not surprisingly, Gene himself brought a small cache of photographs back from Vietnam along with his drawings. Many of the black-and-white images were predictably graphic, painful, and emotionally wrenching scenes depicting the horrors of combat. When he gave them to me for safekeeping I hid them in the converted formal dining room I used as a study so that my seven-year-old twins wouldn't find them. I knew I'd be answering a lot of disturbing questions if they did.

Seeing these photos accomplished something: they started me thinking about the differences between photography and sketch artistry, particularly as they relate to interpreting a war. Even to a non-artist like me, some differences are obvious. For example, the power of photography derives in good part from its inherently faithful depiction of reality. You can alter color or shading or tinting to make a photo more pleasing to the eye. You can crop a scene to focus on a particular message. You can even editorialize by selecting only photos that support a particular point of view while choosing not to shoot, print, or publish those that don't. But ultimately your editorial or narrative options with photography are limited by the reality of the subject material—the happiness a photographer wishes to capture in a scene may be real enough, but if the subjects don't smile for the camera, they won't be smiling in the picture.

The situation is different with a sketch. Whereas a photograph is grounded in objectivity, a sketch always reflects an element of bias. At its unretouched core, a photo shows us "what happened," while a sketch conveys "what I think happened" or maybe even "what should have happened." The concepts of photographic reality versus sketch bias have been widely embraced. They are the reason that news articles are accompanied by photos while sketches adorn the editorials.

It can even be argued that a sketch virtually requires subjective interpretation by the artist. The photographer decides whether a scene tells a story of interest; the camera captures it faithfully. The sketch artist likewise decides whether a scene is of interest, but once chosen, the scene is inevitably altered by the artist. One does not—indeed, one cannot—draw with the realism of a photograph. Consciously or unconsciously, the elements of a sketch are subtly adjusted. Expressions, and therefore emotions, are forged or stylized.

In the end, it is the feeling and mood of a scene—not necessarily its historical accuracy—that is captured by the pen or pencil.

For example, consider a newspaper artist who spends the day watching a man fishing from a boat. If his editor says he can publish just a single scene to convey the experience, how does he depict the day's adventure? The answer depends on many factors. For example:

- What are the facts? Did the fisherman catch a big trout? Or did he get skunked? Did it rain? Did the boat sink?
- From whose perspective is the story told?
    The fisherman's?
    Or the fish's?
- What is the subject's mood?

- Is the fisherman . . .
- Happy?
- Angry?
- Dejected?
- What is the artist's mood? Is he an optimist or a pessimist?
  Does he like fishing or hate it? Did he eat breakfast that day,

or is he hungry? Or tired? Did he have a fight with his wife? Is he bored? Are the mosquitos driving him crazy?

When are photos better for depicting a scene? When are drawings better? Steve Northup, photographer and wartime acquaintance of Gene Basset, offers this insight: "Why limit your questions to photographers or sketchers? Some of the most horrific depictions of battle are carved on the [stone] walls of Angkor Wat. I think the medium an artist brings to the battlefield is pretty immaterial. Anything, short of play-dough, will get the job done. I really don't think there is a 'better' [technique]."

Northup further suggests that the basic differences between sketch art and photography, in terms of their ability to "faithfully depict" reality, may be moot. As he puts it, "We used to believe in the concept of photographic truth, but since the advent of Photoshop that's pretty much gone out the window." These same factors invariably influence the artist as he records scenes from a war; even when he tries to be faithful and accurate, his drawings won't capture reality like a photo because they are inevitably modified by the subject's emotional state, the artist's perspective and mood, and dozens of other factors.

There is one area relevant to Gene's drawings where I feel comfortable claiming to be a true expert. It's an area that, paradoxically, constitutes its own subtle form of art: the art of medicine.

There are many facets to the art of medicine, but none more important than the ability to understand how patients are affected by their infirmity. The patient must be able to cope with his sickness, disability, aging, or even impending death. Regardless of a physician's specialty, one of the most complex yet crucial aspects of medicine is to understand not just how the disease affects the patient, but how the patient reacts to the disease. The Mayo brothers paid their respects to this concept when they proclaimed that, "the needs of the patient come first." Implicit in their words is the idea that you cannot know what the patient needs to cope with his or her illness until you understand how the patient is reacting to his or her illness.

In 1969, this simple concept moved to the forefront of psychiatric thinking with the publication of *On Death and Dying* by Elisabeth Kübler-Ross.[7] The book was an instant cultural phenomenon and, although not without its critics,[8] it still remains an icon of popular psychology.[9]

The Art of Medicine

The practice of medicine is both a science and an art. The science part is easy; having taught at a medical school for decades, I can attest that the most inept first-year students usually learn the scientific part of medicine well enough to eventually practice it. The concept of art, when applied to the practice of medicine, is a loose term and one that's not easy to define. I've had some quality arguments with physicians who insist that there is no art to medicine—that medicine is purely a scientific amalgam of logic and data and technology and skilled hands. I disagree. To me, the practice of medicine hinges on the qualitative, aesthetic things that you do to optimize the care of the patient—how you extract the necessary history, how you explain the problem and your recommendations, how you match a particular therapy to a specific patient's needs and fears (for example, if the science says that a certain problem can be treated with either surgery or radiation or chemotherapy, how do you make sure the patient receives the modality that's best for them?). There are thousands of clinical scenarios like these that cannot be reduced to a scientific formula or cookbook approach, nor for which there is even a right or wrong answer. Asking a doctor "which is a better treatment: an operation or pills?" makes no more sense scientifically than asking an artist "which is a better color: red or blue?" In both cases, the answer depends upon situational and/or patient-specific intangibles, and choosing the best option is the "art." It's the art part of medicine that's hard to master. Doctors trained in the modern age of evidence-based medicine are loath to admit this, but art is a much larger, and far more important, component of medicine than science. (By my biased estimate at least 80 percent of medical practice involves aspects best described as art rather than science.)

Dr. Kübler-Ross, a psychiatrist working at the University of Chicago, refined her theories during the height of the Vietnam War. More than forty years later, her general hypothesis is familiar to anyone who's ever taken a high school or college course in psychology. Briefly, Kübler-Ross studied how people react to the psychological trauma of death (either their own impending death, or the death of others). She came to the conclusion that the grieving process follows five more-or-less predictable steps: denial, anger, bargaining, depression, and acceptance. In short order, her concept of "The Five Stages of Grief" was applied to other types of loss: it's not hard to picture someone progressing through each of the stages as they react to the loss of a loved one, the loss of a job, the discovery that their significant other is cheating, or even something as seemingly minor as an unexpected bad grade at school. One can easily envision how a young soldier's military experience could eventually engender all five steps in the grieving process.

The Kübler-Ross model of grieving is, admittedly, simplistic. Some have even called its basic validity into question. Other approaches to grief resolution have been hypothesized (for example, see *A Grief Observed* by C. S. Lewis, or *The Soul in Grief* by Robert Romanyshyn). Indeed, even Kübler-Ross herself came to accept the limitations of her approach later in life after suffering a debilitating

5. *A Young Draftee's Journey through the Kübler-Ross Stages of Grief.*
    In a drawing made almost fifty years after the war, Gene reminds the viewer that the five-step progression from denial through acceptance is not necessarily rapid. In this particular case, the journey takes many years.

stroke in 1995. She cowrote another book—*On Grief and Grieving*—which revisited many of the themes she had published earlier, and she concluded somewhat reluctantly that her own recent struggle with grief (and depression) had involved "so much more than the five stages."[10] Today there is considerable skepticism in the psychiatric community regarding her five stage approach, and grieving is now recognized to be far more complex than she had originally proposed.[11] It is widely accepted that you don't always deny, become angry, bargain, feel depressed, or accept your way through five distinct stages of grief. The process is not, as Kübler-Ross eventually wrote in *On Grief and Grieving*, written in stone. Instead:

> The five stages . . . are part of the framework that makes up our learning to live with the one we lost. They are tools to help us frame and identify what we may be feeling. But they are not stops on some linear timeline in grief. Not everyone goes through all of

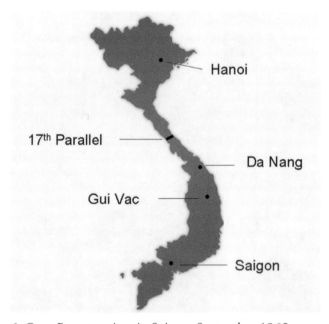

6. Gene Basset arrives in Saigon, September 1965.

"I spent almost three months traversing a great deal of South Vietnam, from the rice paddies of the Mekong Delta to the 17th Parallel, on an aircraft carrier, a river patrol junk, a Coast Guard cutter, and patrols with the Green Berets in the Golden Triangle, rich with opium trade."

them or goes in a prescribed order . . . Our hope is that with these stages comes the knowledge of grief's terrain, making us better equipped to cope with life and loss.

This is how we can use the Kübler-Ross stages of grief—as a framework around which grief can be hung out and examined. No, this is not a rigid structure without flexibility. Yes, there is room here for reinterpretation, alternative analyses, and even frank dissent. Despite its flaws there is a practical utility to the Kübler-Ross model that, even today, can prove valuable. It is this utility that can hopefully be employed as a means for organizing and exploring Gene's drawings.

Even though I'm an internist, not a psychiatrist, I nevertheless learned to recognize and understand the Kübler-Ross five stages of grief because so many of my own patients pass through these stages at some point in their illness. Patients get unpleasant news, receive bad diagnoses, experience therapeutic setbacks, suffer side effects, feel pain, etc. As a result, they grieve. It's my job to recognize their reactions to grief—reactions that may include denial, anger, bargaining,

7. Gene pauses to capture an impromptu scene. Photograph by Koichi Sawada. Courtesy of Gene Basset.

depression, and acceptance—and deal with them. This doesn't necessarily involve a lot of science, but it does involve a lot of art.

I believe that grief explains the powerful emotional impact found in Gene's simple, understated sketches from Vietnam. One evening, years ago, I was staring at his drawings and realized something important: What is the message here? Why are the sketches so compelling? The answer suddenly seemed clear—they take the viewer on a wartime journey through Kübler-Ross's five stages of grief. Gene's drawings reveal the war-related grieving of soldiers as well as the Vietnamese people, and even the subtle grieving of the artist himself. Relying on nothing more than my own impressions, I was quickly able to sort all of Gene's war drawings into those depicting denial, anger, bargaining, depression, and acceptance. There was nothing forced or contrived about this process; although they didn't physically

8. Gene amuses local children with his drawings. Photograph by Steve Northup. Courtesy of Gene Basset.

Politics, Opinions, and the War

Gene's visit to Vietnam didn't just generate the drawings that form the basis for this book; they provided material for years of political interpretation and commentary (for example, the following cartoon appeared on the front page of Scripps Howard's *Washington Daily News*. It bears the caption "We have turned the corner . . ." But what are Gene's stated political inclinations, and how were they affected by his time in Vietnam? I asked him these questions directly.

Q: Did you have strong political beliefs before you went to Vietnam?

GENE: Maybe. I was familiar with Communism, that's for certain. My introduction to Communism was through a few relatives. But as an artist, freedom was fundamental and I found it had no room in this ideology. Far left or far right does not allow for an open mind. Supporters of the war were questioning the patriotism of others. I was also affected by this same philosophy (although not directly) by the practice of blacklisting in the 1950s.

Q: Did you have a lot of preconceived notions about the war before you left?

GENE: I really don't think so. The folks at Scripps Howard were, of course, in favor of the war. At that time I'd followed it a little bit and I had an impression that the war was wrong, but I wasn't adamant about it. I definitely didn't have any preconceived agenda. Frankly, I didn't understand the war, and I looked at this as an educational opportunity to learn more. Look, I was an editorial and political cartoonist. I made my living taking positions on issues, poking fun at things, lampooning . . . but I always felt that I was looking at—and sketching—this war with an impartial mind.

Q: What did your friends who had already been to Vietnam tell you about the scene there?

GENE: At that time I really didn't know anybody who'd been there. The first person I talked to who knew anything first-hand about the war was a reporter named Jim Lucas. He'd won a Pulitzer Prize in 1954 for his work in Korea, and I remember that he was very much "pro war" back then. I knew him as a war correspondent, but we really didn't meet up and talk much until I got to Vietnam. We roomed together in Saigon for a short while after I arrived. The two of us traveled around together—mostly Saigon and Da Nang—for several days, and we spent some time together on a cutter at sea. I think we overlapped about two weeks. He got me settled in—and gave me my earliest firsthand information and opinions about what was going on there.

Q: So did you form an opinion about the war while you there?

GENE: Definitely. I went off with a sketchbook, a camera, and an open mind. But by the time I got back I knew the war was wrong, and along the way I realized that the "snap shots" I was drawing would be my story.

9. The war comes home.

This January 31, 1968, Gene Basset cartoon appeared on the front page of the *Washington Daily News* (a Scripps Howard newspaper). The caption reads, "We have turned the corner."

move like the planchette on a Ouija board, Gene's pictures practically sorted themselves into the five categories. Just as importantly, they did so with an ease and certainty that convinced me Gene had subconsciously appreciated the grief around him and had sketched people working their way through this grief. I say subconsciously because Gene has always denied any conscious awareness that he was experiencing or capturing these emotions. "I had no concept of 'grief resolution' at that time; I was not involved with concepts like 'love' or 'happiness' as I drew. So I wasn't trying to explore or depict it, or anything else. I didn't try to insert emotions when they weren't there. There was nothing contrived. Ever."

There's a lesson here, and photographer Steve Northup nails it. When asked whether it made any sense to send someone like Gene Basset to Vietnam, he offers his usual clear insight into the role of the correspondent, photographer, or artist:

> The goal is to inform the home front. When a nation goes to war, it spends three things: the gold of its treasury, the blood of its children, and its good name. I've never trusted the officials, who are doing the spending, to report accurately on their/our investments. I'm not sure a terrified twenty-something is a better solution, but it's tough to get the middle-aged onto the battlefield. . . . As to which I'd send, I'd pick the person with the strongest heart.

But if it's "tough to get the middle-aged onto the battlefield," who do you send to cover the war? Gene was that man, the guy with the "strongest heart," the one who didn't want to see a repeat of the mistakes—and, by extension, the grief—of the past. I believe that in 1965 he (subconsciously) sketched an army, a country, and even himself dealing with the grief spawned by the Vietnam War. Through his drawings (and the figure legends/comments he provides for each) Gene not only "informed the home front" but also taught a lesson about the inseparability of grief from war that anyone—even a simple midwestern blood-vessel doctor—can appreciate. It's a lesson we can relearn, almost fifty years later, by revisiting the delicate, sensitive sketches Gene carried back with him from the most indelicate, insensitive place he would ever visit.

Acknowledgments

The author would like to acknowledge the many, many contributions that his wife, Julie Rooke, has made to this work—and to just about everything else I've ever written.

Julie, I am both appreciative of and, frankly, awed by your unparalleled editing skills, invaluable insight, and unwavering support. On behalf of myself—and the countless other writers with whom you've worked and for whom you've been the key to a successful publication—I offer a sincere thank-you for every pound of help and guidance you've given us.

Gene Basset's Acknowledgments

After a tumultuous C-123 ride, with pigs running loose in the cabin and cows about to join in, I arrived in Gia Vuc at Detachment A-103, 5th Special Forces Group of the First Special Forces in Vietnam, and was greeted by, "Oh no. Another artist." My predecessor was Howard Brodie, the famed combat artist of World War II, Korea, Indochina, and Vietnam. He had to be medevacked because of dysentery. I assured the Green Berets that I was relatively healthy and was accepted without any noticeable qualms.

To Capt. William Hicks, Linden, NC; Sgt. Tony Tantalo, Waterloo, NY; Sgt. Norm Bircher, Topeka, KS; Sgt. James Harrison, Baltimore, MD; Sgt. Charles Minnicks, McKeesport, PA; and Sgt. Lloyd Littlel, Hickory, NC, for great camaraderie and for keeping me alive.

To Jim Lucas, companion of Robert Capa and Pulitzer Prize winner for his dispatches from the Korean War, for sharing his knowledge of Indochina and providing guidance when I first arrived.

To Earl Richert, my boss at Scripps Howard, and Editor-in-Chief, Walker Stone, who sent me to Vietnam even though we disagreed on the justification of the war.

To Steve Northup, UPI photographer, who shared his deep and thoughtful insights into the politics and culture of Vietnam.

To Dr. Thom Rooke, my collaborator, who gave—and gives—life and understanding.

To Julie Rooke, Thom's wife, the provider of the glue, whose editing put the whole thing together.

To my wife, Ann, who helped elicit forgotten anecdotes from my sketchbooks, with thoughtful suggestions and patience!

Gene Basset's Vietnam Sketchbook

1

Denial

Gene Basset sat in the warm evening air atop the Majestic Hotel in downtown Saigon. Joining him at the rooftop restaurant were three old friends, all photographers sent by various parties to cover the war in Vietnam. Eddie Adams would win a Pulitzer Prize in 1969 for his photo of *General Nguyen Ngoc Loan executing a Viet Cong prisoner in Saigon*. Henri Huet would capture some of the best-known scenes of the war before dying in a helicopter crash over Laos in 1971. Steve Northup would become a successful photographer, author, and Harvard University Neiman Fellow. But these milestones lay somewhere off in the future. At this moment, four friends were simply enjoying a gourmet open-air dinner in a lovely urban setting. The war, at least for now, did not exist. Had the scene been photographed at this precise instant, the caption might have easily read, "War? What war?"

Steve Northup described the feelings that evening:

> A few words about the friendship shared by Eddie, Henri and myself. They were Associated Press staff photographers; I was a staff guy for United Press International. While we were supposed to be rivals, we were, in fact, good and close friends, bound by mutual respect and the terrible things we had to photograph. As wire service photographers, we were responsible for what a great chunk of the world saw of the war. At the same time we were anonymous. The photographs that emerged from our old Leicas were seen across the planet, but carried only the byline *AP photo* or *UPI photo*. We were used to seeing each other in jungle fatigues, dirty and tired. This evening was different: clean clothes, fine food, a bit of wine and going home to sleep between clean sheets. A serious luxury.

But not a luxury destined to be enjoyed for long. Just before the entrée was served, the horizon abruptly erupted with an incendiary glow and the unmistakable staccato of automatic guns blazing away

10. *Rude Interruption.*
    My first night in Saigon involved a rooftop dinner at the Majestic Hotel, which was interrupted by loud explosions and a firefight on the edge of town.

with harmful intentions. A firefight. Gene set down his soupspoon and quickly sketched *Rude Interruption*. The violent outburst shattered the calm that had graced the meal seconds earlier, but more importantly it forced the al fresco diners to quickly reacquaint themselves with reality. The chance to serve up another steaming, tasty bowl of denial before confronting a cold, bland main course of "Hey, buddy—haven't you noticed that there's a nasty war going on out there?" was gone for the night.

Denial is a classic psychiatric defense mechanism in which an individual refuses to acknowledge certain painful aspects of reality.[1] Sigmund Freud gets a healthy share of the credit for developing the concept. Freud argued that there are distinct (although not necessarily anatomically defined) aspects of the brain that deal with pleasure, reality, and morality. He called these theoretical cerebral entities the id, ego, and superego, and he postulated that they continuously battle one another for psychic dominance. Humans are thus perpetually torn between a lust for hedonistic stimulations like sex and violence (id) and the restraint on this lust imposed by their conscience (super-ego). Rational thought and logic (the ego) act as the referee in this fracas. The ensuing battle creates psychological conflict. Conflict produces anxiety. Ultimately, this anxiety must be dealt with. But how?

Freud maintained that individuals develop various means to cope with conflict and, more importantly, the anxiety it produces; he called these means "defense mechanisms." According to Freud, denial is a key defense mechanism. By denying that something has occurred (or by denying that it might occur) the subject temporarily avoids the stress of dealing with it. The practical dilemma, of course, is that denial doesn't resolve psychological conflict—it merely postpones the need to deal with it. And denial is only useful in small doses. Deny reality a little and people think you're eccentric. But deny reality too much and you find yourself facedown in a white rubber room on the receiving end of a Thorazine drip.

It's an old joke that "Denial ain't just a river in Egypt." This well-worn adage has been widely attributed to Mark Twain (although it's pure fiction—there is no reputable source for this claim), who achieved fame for his writings shortly before Freud achieved fame for his psychoanalytic theories. Regardless of whether he actually said it or not, Twain was a well-read man with eclectic interests that included science and medicine; although Freud did not specifically write about denial until shortly after Twain's death.

Freud and his theories are considered dated by many modern psychiatrists,[2] but the entity he called *denial* remains a well-recognized, widely accepted response to stress, conflict, and anxiety—and it's also the first stage in the grieving process, according to Kübler-Ross. Deal successfully with the denial and you can move on to anger, bargaining, and eventually, conflict resolution. Fail to get past the denial stage (or any of the stages) and you'll wander aimlessly in psychological limbo, unable to move beyond the terrible things that have happened.

It's not easy to capture "denial" in a sketch, because many behaviors that look like denial can actually be caused by something else, although Gene claims that technically he can do it. "I can exaggerate a picture enough to convey any emotion or message." For example, in *Cheap Haircut*, a soldier sits with his feet propped up and his guard down as he gets a haircut from a Vietnamese barber. How can the young GI be so relaxed in the midst of the combat, injury, and death threatening to engulf him? Is this denial? Or something else? Consider

11. *Cheap Haircut.*

Many of the soldiers stationed at the military base in Da Nang pre-
ferred to get their hair cut by the numerous professional barbers in the city,
who could do a job that was more satisfactory than the grooming received
on base. Most of the Vietnamese barbers also did a certain amount of chi-
ropractic work for their customers, not only trimming their hair but also
adjusting the alignment of their necks and backs.

the possibilities. Has the trauma of war left him wounded by grief? If so, perhaps he's quietly working through Kübler-Ross–style war-related denial on his way to the next stages of conflict resolution? Or has his mind snapped from the stress of combat, leaving him incapable of even acknowledging that he's engulfed in a war? Is he just extraordinarily naïve and simply doesn't understand the dangers lurking everywhere? Maybe he comprehends that there's a war going on but he doesn't believe the consequences will affect him? Or does he understand his precarious situation but ignores the danger because he thinks the only thing that can hurt him is Kryptonite?[3] For an artist striving to be objective in his work, it may not be possible to discern these differences. Gene recognizes this limitation and makes no attempt to interpret the scene. When asked directly whether he thought the kid getting a haircut was "in denial or just indifferent," Gene responded with equal directness. "It could be denial. I don't know. I couldn't tell by looking at him. I don't think anybody could. I recall just having visited a nearby barber before I made this sketch. I got a haircut and had my neck cracked as part of the session. Seeing this GI having 'my experience,' I thought it was more blissful ignorance for the moment."

So there's denial, and there are things that look like denial.[4] Gene unconsciously explores the broad spectrum and potentially subtle differences between denial and important look-alikes, such as ignorance and disregard, in his next four drawings.

Lest there be any confusion about the message in *You're Kidding? This Is Our Relief?*, the anonymous corporal's words—"You're kidding . . . ?"—hammer home the point: I'm in denial here. This scene doesn't try to show us the dark, pathological type of denial that might eventually end in insanity, nor the (mostly) healthy form of denial that sets the wounded soul down the Kübler-Ross road to grief resolution. What's captured here is more appropriately called "disbelief," something that's akin to the curiously amusing emotion that hapless Wile E. Coyote demonstrates every time he falls (predictably) off a cliff. Here, the khaki-clad old-timers watching a herd of new troops stampede off the transport plane can't believe that these underage, undisciplined misfits are somehow supposed to relieve them. We smile to ourselves at these disbelieving veterans, knowing that their "You're kidding . . ." moment of incredulous denial will quickly give way to a similar semi-serious burst of bargaining ("I'd give anything for some guys with a little fight in 'em . . ."), anger ("Who's idea of a joke was it to send us this batch of goofballs . . ."), etc. We can even predict with confidence that the scene will eventual progress sitcom-style to acceptance ("Well, I suppose we'll just have to make-do with these pimple-packing teenage bozos for now . . ."). Gene isn't trying for pathos here; he knows that the cartoonish disbelief shown in *"You're Kidding . . ."* is such a universal response that it will be easily recognized for what it is and appreciated by his civilian audience back home.

In contrast, *Where the Elite Meet to Eat if You Speak French* suggests that denial is not the only thing that can cause indifferent behavior. Maybe a person simply doesn't understand the significance of things happening around them? In this drawing, the pampered French wife of a wealthy rubber-plantation owner prepares to enjoy an elegant meal; she sits with her back to the viewer and seems as oblivious to the events occurring outside the window as she is to the exorbitant price of her upcoming lunch. On first impression one might attribute her apparent indifference to denial about the war and its consequences. But is this really denial? Maybe she simply doesn't care? Or doesn't realize what's happening around her? Perhaps the extreme isolation of plantation life—and her protected, regal lifestyle—have combined to shelter her from the reality of war? Could the fact that she speaks only French mean that she doesn't talk with the locals about current affairs? Is lunch at the Continental Palace the most—or perhaps only—contact she has with the real world? We wonder if this genteel lady is someone who, because of social position, geographic isolation, language barriers, etc., does not actually understand the situation with regard to the ongoing war. In the bluntest of terms, she might appear to be exhibiting classic signs of denial, but in this case perhaps her apparent indifference means that she is merely ignorant of the problems around her. When asked for his opinion regarding her state of mind, Gene is quick to clarify. "My immediate intention was to simply contrast two dramatically different social situations. The woman inside the restaurant is speaking French to a French-schooled Vietnamese waiter. Other than her servants, my guess is that she had little contact with people like the woman passing by."

In *Mass Transit* and *Shepherd in the Field* we see another way in which certain behaviors can mimic denial—by blatantly disregarding danger rather than denying it exists. *Mass Transit* depicts two denizens of the city puttering about on their motorized rickshaw

12. *"You're Kidding, This Is Our Relief?"* 1965.

This image from Gia Vuc reflects the frustration of the disciplined Green Berets with the mercenary soldiers recruited (some Montagnards, some from Saigon and elsewhere) by the South Vietnamese. The group of new arrivals appears unprepared; one carries a guitar while another is accompanied by a pet dog. The plane from which they emerge, labeled "UNITED STATES ARMY," is a "caribou" military transport, useful for its ability to land on a fairly short airstrip. The ironic sign labeled "LBJ RANCH" has images of a cow and a pig, common livestock in the region. The ink on this sketch, and others, ran when I fell into the stream during a fire fight.

while purposefully ignoring the war lurking just outside the cartoon frame. It's "business as usual" for the aloof couple as they motor through confusion and chaos.

Shepherd in the Field shows a less kinetic form of disregard. Here, a young shepherd, likely asleep beneath his high, wide hat, makes no

13. *Where the Elite Meet to Eat If You Speak French.*
Continental Palace Hotel.

The Continental Palace was the grand old French hotel in Saigon, and was where I, along with my colleague from Scripps Howard, correspondent Jim Lucas, stayed upon first arriving in Vietnam. The hotel's restaurant was sophisticated, and was still at that time frequented by French plantation owners in Vietnam. The cuisine and service were both Continental, and the waiter dressed in formal bow tie. It also presents a contrast between the inside, European-based world and its relative wealth, and the outside, with a less-affluent Vietnamese person struggling to carry a load.

14. *Mass Transit.*

    This street scene shows the relative confusion of all the motorized rickshaws—powered by fuel from Esso (now Exxon)—which required that each driver negotiate passage, since there were no traffic cops to control the situation.

effort to hide his disinterest. As long as the war doesn't force him to respond, this is one shepherd boy who is going to keep on ignoring it.

I interviewed a Vietnamese woman at Mayo Clinic who was a nurse during the war. While describing the rural village in which she had grown up, she was struck by the similarities between the boy in *Shepherd* and her younger brother, who also tended the family's buffalo (in a sisterly way, she pointed out that her brother was a virtual Zen master when it came to ignoring things). She related a brief conversation her brother once held with a passing newspaper reporter (loose translation):

WAR CORRESPONDENT: How do you deal with all the danger around here?

SHEPHERD (sitting in the same fashion as the boy in the picture. He looks up, sleepily): I try not to think about it.

CORRESPONDENT: There are land mines here. What if you step on one?

SHEPHERD: If you step on one, you die. Or wind up with only one leg. I try not to think about it.

CORRESPONDENT: What about that fellow with the gun over there. He's guarding you and the village against raiders from the hills. What if he steps on a mine?

SHEPHERD: If he gets blown up, bandits and soldiers are going to wander down here and steal everything. I try not to think about it.

CORRESPONDENT: What if your buffalo steps on a mine?

SHEPHERD: (Pauses, looks up. A small smile crosses his face.) If that happens there will be one less mine for the rest of us to step on. And we will feast for the next few weeks.

CORRESPONDENT: So . . . do you ever think about that?

SHEPHERD: All the time.

Denial is commonly used to describe a wide range of thoughts and behaviors, only a few of which have psychiatric implications. *Latest Black Market Shipment* illustrates one of these variants of denial. Two soldiers stride through a collection of illegal black-market stalls, their deadpan faces arguing silently that, "There's nothing to see here. Let's move on." Psychologists describe this type of thinking as denial of fact, a form of denial in which someone avoids reality by lying (to themselves as well as others) about the truth.[5] By

15. *Shepherd in the Field.*

This was drawn in the highlands inhabited by the Montagnards, the Vietnamese mountain people who were recruited as paid mercenary soldiers. The buffalo in the region served two purposes, both as agrarian animals and also to help find the land mines left over from the French, who left behind no maps of the mine locations. When a buffalo stepped on a mine and was killed, the immediate area was then considered to be relatively safe.

I stayed in the village of Gia Vuc for three weeks. Located on the border with Cambodia and Laos, it was in the so-called Golden Triangle, which harbored much of the drug trade, especially in poppies. An armed man in the background keeps watch out over the hills.

denying the obvious, these suddenly near-sighted soldiers convince themselves that "nothing is wrong" with the world around them.[6]

Contrast this to the message in *Loading Up for Hanoi*, a look at neurotic (as opposed to psychotic) thinking.[7] The scene focuses on a carrier-based plane being loaded for a bombing run against the North. I work with a radiologist at the Mayo Clinic who spent his

16. *Latest Black Market Shipment.*

The black market flourished in Vietnam and was very lucrative for those in control of it. Many items that were scarce at the military base, such as cigarettes, could be purchased more cheaply through such illicit but unchecked means.

Vietnam years loading bombs just like the men in the sketch. When asked to comment on Gene's drawing, the doctor observed that:

> I was too young, or more probably unaware/naïve, to really appreciate what was going on politically during the Vietnam era. I was sent there to do a job. I didn't think much about where the bombs would be dropped or on whom they would land. I only knew it felt good to load the aircraft, finish the task, and watch it take off. The planes would come back empty and then we knew we'd done our job correctly. It was on to the next aircraft. Twelve hours on, twelve hours off. Seven days a week, one day off a month. Endless piles of bombs to load; one day pretty much like the next . . .
>
> I didn't think about the politics or killing. I just needed to load the bombs.[8]

BASSET
ABOARD THE CARRIER
BON HOMME
RICHARD

17. *Loading Up for Hanoi.*

I sketched crew members aboard the carrier *Bon Homme Richard* during the start of the bombing of the North.

The subjects in *Loading Up for Hanoi* don't likewise "think about" certain realities. They know that they put the bombs on the plane. That the planes drop them on something—or someone. And that the planes come back for more. Unfortunately, it's psychologically punishing to confront these facts on a daily basis; it's easier if you don't think about them. The result is denial of consequences ("What? Those bombs I loaded on the planes landed on people?"). Similar psychological tools include minimization (recognizing the truth while denying its seriousness or impact)[9] and rationalization (recognizing the truth but coming up with ingenious arguments to justify your actions—think of it as psychiatric shorthand for "making up excuses").

Unwinding from a Trip to Hanoi and *Time Out for a Cuban Cigar* explore additional forms of denial. Both drawings depict soldiers on break between combat engagements. It's not hard to imagine elements of the various conversations that might be occurring in these scenes or how they could reflect various denial-related defense mechanisms:

> "I don't hate the Viet Cong. They hate me."
> *(Denial through Projection)*
> "I didn't want to bomb anybody, but orders are orders."
> *(Denial of Responsibility)*
> "It was dark when the shooting started, so we probably missed everything. I bet no one got hurt."
> *(Denial of Impact)*

The presence of alcohol in these scenes reminds the viewer of yet another spin on denial: so-called denial of awareness, in which the subject denies being aware of the truth because they were intoxicated, asleep, or otherwise impaired at the time of the events.[10]

Polite fiction is another form of denial. With polite fiction, people behave as if things are normal—even when everyone knows that they're not. The problem is that no one will speak the obvious. A classic example of polite fiction occurred on a national scale in the 1950s when schoolchildren practiced for atomic-bomb attacks by ducking under their desks and covering their heads. It was a most pathetic and desperate form of deception, an activity meant to give people hope that their children might survive an atomic attack when

18. *Unwinding from a Trip to Hanoi.*
    At the Marine Officers' Club in Da Nang, Marine flyers tell of their bombing raids up north earlier that day. The Marines, among them the captain at the lower left, are served drinks by noncommissioned servicemen.

19. *Time Out for a Cuban Cigar.*

I was welcomed at Junk Base II by these servicemen, Lieutenant Tamony and Boatswain's Mate A. C. Smith, who were surprised to encounter an artist. The base was one of several along the streams that fed into the South China Sea. Patrols were frequently made from such bases, searching for contraband moving along the Ho Chi Minh Trail, which makes the soldiers' possession of the Cuban cigars rather ironic. It was also at this base that I recall one of my best meals ever in Vietnam, prepared over a charcoal pot by a French-trained Vietnamese cook who served the base. Many of the servicemen there did not care for Vietnamese food and did not appreciate the delicious fish dinner I found so appealing.

everyone—children included—knew perfectly well that they weren't going to avoid annihilation by hiding under the desk.[11]

Gene illustrates polite fiction in *Follow the Leader . . . Green Beret Sgt.* The sergeant leads his ragtag crew of local recruits with the same look of determined commitment he'd have if he were marching with a whole platoon of elite Special Forces behind him. The "troops" keep up the illusion, maintaining as much seriousness and dignity as their sandals and ill-fitting uniforms will allow. To the observer of this amusing scene, it seems that everyone is pretending this outfit is combat worthy solely for the sake of appearances.

In 1967, Paul McCartney wrote a song for the Beatles entitled "The Fool on the Hill." Two years earlier, Gene sketched *South Viet*

20. *Follow the Leader . . . Green Beret Sgt.*

An image of the discrepancy between the American Green Beret and the group of Montagnards he leads out on patrol. The American puffs on a cigar, clad in proper military garb, while his followers tag along, some outfitted with boots, but at least one in zories, the often-seen Vietnamese sandals, which provide little protection for the feet.

Gunboat off the 17th Parallel or, as some have called it, "The Fool on the Hull." There is, of course, nothing in the drawing to suggest that the man reclining against the cabin of the vessel is actually a "fool" other than the silly smirk Gene has captured. And what a leering mug! Doesn't this guy get it? There's a war going on, so why the goofy grin? Is this ignorance? Probably not. This sailor surely understands the seriousness of his situation; we know that he knows that (1) combat could erupt just up the coast, and (2) when the shooting starts, a small wooden junk probably isn't the safest place to be standing. Likewise, this isn't minimization, rationalization, or polite fiction either. This is defiance. Defiance can be teamed with aggression, which is what we see in *Untitled*. Here, the *Fool on the Hull* has struck a fierce, bold, insolent pose—he's become Rambo and he's practically begging the enemy to take their best shot at him. *Rev up the engines, boys—we're going in.*

The nautical theme continues with *Keeping the Cutter Shipshape* and *Patrol*, two scenes depicting sailors as they toil aboard the USS

21. *South Viet Gunboat off the 17th Parallel.*
This drawing was made on the cutter *Point Welcome* as a junk was passing by just off the coast of Vietnam.

22. *Untitled.*

"You will find peace not by trying to escape your problems, but by confronting them courageously. You will find peace not in denial, but in victory." — J. Donald Waters

Point Welcome. In these sketches, Gene offers up yet another variant on the theme of "denial look-alikes"—in this case, the message is: "there might be a war going on, but we're too busy to care."

Gene depicts another denial-related entity—deception—in *Passing Ships* and *Protecting Saigon—Called the White Mice. Passing Ships* shows an encounter between Gene's cutter and an unidentified destroyer—unidentified, but possibly the very ship that was fired upon in 1964 during the Gulf of Tonkin incident! Gene describes that the cutter, the USS *Point Welcome* would unload a couple of harmless rounds, and the North would reply in kind. Gene almost casually adds that, "A year before, the Gulf of Tonkin incident of a false report of an attack on a U.S. destroyer was the excuse for bombing the North," and by doing so reminds the viewer that "lying" and "denial" are not such different things. The artist is unapologetic as he infers a not-so-subtle link between the Department of Defense lie he claims gave birth to the war and the official government denials of the Gulf of Tonkin events that haunted it for decades to follow.

23. USS *Point Welcome,* 1965. Photo courtesy of Gene Basset.

Perhaps the most powerful and tragic form of denial occurs when we deny who we are. The biblical mob scene in which Peter denies knowing Jesus is a classic and particularly poignant example. Gene illustrates his own version of the convergence between lies and denial in *Protecting Saigon—Called the White Mice.* Gene captures the "Mice"—ostensibly protective police, but actually government spies—as they patrol the city streets of the capitol. Basset learned about their hidden role firsthand: "While I stayed at the Continental Palace hotel, the White Mice went through the belongings in my room. I made friends with the houseboys after I had drawn caricatures of them. They tipped me off about the White Mice." His depiction of "Mice" leaves no room for interpretation; the men in this picture won't look you in the eye as they dawdle uneasily on the street corner; they are fearful that you'll see through them and their deception. In *Protecting Saigon,* Gene sketches a portrait of deceit, lies, and—ultimately—denial in its most depressing form.

We conclude our journey down denial with a final stop. Gene has cracked open the denial piñata to show us everything from "cartoonish disbelief" to "lying spies denying that they are lying spies,"

Text in image: GRENADES HAND FRAG / GREN / BASSET COAST GUARD CUTTER POINT WELCOME

24. *Keeping the Cutter Shipshape*.

During a down time aboard the cutter *Point Welcome*, the crew was ordered to spiff up the vessel, including painting it darker gray for camouflage, so that when it returned to Da Nang Harbor it would be shipshape. In the background can be seen a hillside with houses, indicating how close to shore the ship was traveling, and near to the soldiers are boxes with hand grenades.

BASSET
COAST GUARD
CUTTER POINT
WELCOME

25. *Patrol*.

This drawing indicates the bustle of activity aboard the *Point Welcome*.

The Coast Guard emblem can be seen on the vessel, and the American flag flies above.

26. *Passing Ships.*
    The comings and goings involved in patrolling the coastline.

but the most important form of denial has not yet been depicted. It's the type of denial introduced at the opening of this chapter, the painful psychological denial that instantly follows bad news, the "Dear God, no . . . it can't be" moment when reality first dawns on you. It's the reason for writing this chapter. And this book. Fortunately, Gene does not disappoint. He gives us *Minor Wound*.

Minor Wound captures perfectly the denial described by Kübler-Ross. Here, we see a soldier who has sustained some type of wound in combat. It's not serious, but he doesn't know it yet. All he knows is that he's been injured. He hurts. He may be dying. And the look on his face tells us exactly what he's thinking: *This ain't happening. No way.*

27. *Protecting Saigon—Called the White Mice.*

The "White Mice" were ostensibly charged with policing Saigon but were actually spies for the South Vietnamese. Their white uniforms gave them their nickname, and some of their members questioned me at my hotel on more than one occasion.

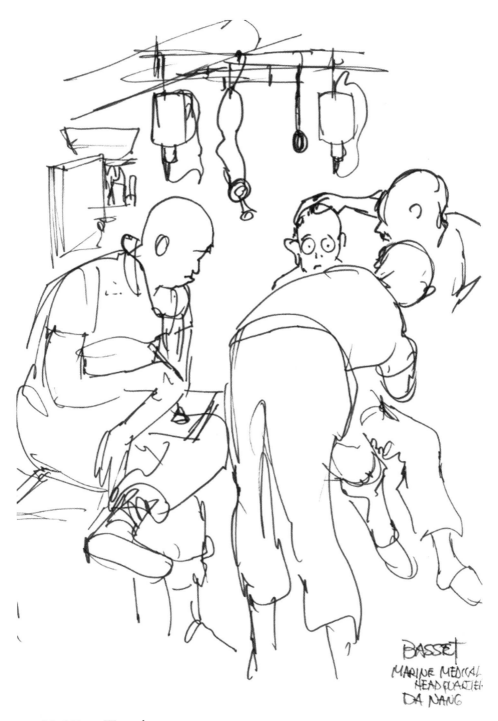

28. *Minor Wound.*

    Although his wound was not serious, the young soldier depicted is wide-eyed with concern and perhaps fear as he is treated by medics.

2

Anger

If the consequences of war produce grief, then Kübler-Ross's model predicts that Gene was going to see and feel a lot of anger during his wartime visit to Vietnam. Is anyone shocked that this prediction came true?

But you don't have to be a war participant working through the grieving process to feel angry. Anger is ubiquitous. Consider something as seemingly innocuous as the act of driving a car. Each year more than half of all drivers admit that they lose their tempers behind the wheel, and the overwhelming majority report experiencing acts of violent highway aggression perpetrated against them by others. Over half of all fatal crashes may involve "aggressive" driving.[1] What's behind this insanity? Justifiable reactions to bad drivers? Doubtful. No, the real factors behind highway anger are a bad day at the office, a fight with the wife, greetings from the IRS, or any of 10,000 other annoyances that routinely irk us.

Generalized anger. According to forensic psychologist and anger guru Dr. Stephen Diamond, "we must acknowledge that some anger is . . . valid, necessary, appropriate, and unavoidable . . . It is not a question of whether we experience anger as much as how we deal with it."[2] I doubt the Dalai Lama agrees with this assessment, but if it's true, then the same observation might be made about excessive drinking, televised football, and work—these things are also arguably "valid, necessary, appropriate, and unavoidable." Perhaps it makes more sense to ask a slightly different but nonetheless simple question: "what causes anger?"

The question may be simple, but the answer is not. Dr. Thomas Stuttaford, a commentator for the London *Times*, suggests that the principal reasons for anger are both vague and, paradoxically, complex. "It is all too easy to attribute (anger) to overcrowding, lack of a stable family, a crumbling community life and the absence of a settled career structure and job security, together with increasing disparity between the rich and poor—all factors that contribute to feelings of deprivation, personal inadequacy, and low self-esteem."[3] Look no further than the first example cited—overcrowding. It's obvious that humans, like rats and wolves, are territorial creatures. If you threaten our turf, we'll get angry. Pack us too tightly together and we'll start fighting each other.

If, as Stuttaford claims, overcrowding is one of the many stresses that can lead to anger, then it's no surprise that this chapter opens with a scene of congested Vietnamese traffic. In *Rush Hour*, Gene takes the viewer to the edge of the urban battlefield and reminds them about a source of anger found in the big cities of every industrialized country on Earth: road rage.[4] There may be a military war going on in the jungle, but the artist points out that there's also a civilian war raging in the streets. This is a war fought in a slow-moving killing field called "traffic," a war waged with mopeds and rickshaws rather than guns—a war in which the combatants are no less angry than those shooting at each other in the countryside. If this automotive sprawl and crawl looks familiar, maybe it's because every motorist since the invention of the internal combustion engine has experienced this same conflict.

In *Rush Hour*, Basset doesn't depict classic road rage. There are no screaming, club-wielding maniacs here. These clenched-jaw motorists stew uneasily, without resorting to obscene gestures. Not yet, anyway. The man on the moped with a cigarette in his mouth, the man driving the Jeep and his passenger, the troops riding in the back of the truck—each character simmers in the pressure cooker of congested traffic, ready to blow like a geyser at the slightest provocation. The artist does not need to show us how the consequences of anger will ultimately erupt down the road; we already know an eruption is coming, and we know the resulting scene might become ugly.

While an angry subject can surely flip the bird in a figurative sense, Gene also acknowledges a literal interpretation for flipping the bird. *Cockfight* depicts one of the oldest and most brutal forms of mass entertainment—combat to the death between two beings. It's a forceful reminder that anger is constantly bubbling beneath our thin veneer of humanity. This anger, the artist suggests, fuels the type of perverse spectator sport shown here. For some, there's a certain sick pleasure to be derived from watching the angry feathered

29. Rush Hour.

Uncontrolled traffic on the streets of Saigon: rickshaws being pedaled, a military convoy, a taxi made by the French Citroën firm (and left over from the period of French occupation of Vietnam), and people on mopeds. I almost never saw just a single person on a moped—there was usually at least a second person as a passenger.

combatants topple and kill each other, just as there was once a certain sick pleasure in watching gladiators do the same to one another in the Coliseum. With this scene, Gene reminds us of our uniquely human capacity to find diversion in, of all things, combat and ritualized death. He unconsciously points out that, if this passes for sport, maybe we shouldn't be so surprised that there's a whole lot of anger and killing taking place in that rice paddy over there?

Anger between noncombatants. *Rush Hour* is a reminder that one doesn't need to be at war to feel angry. Tension, irritation, and frustration are universal, and there's no shortage of vague enemies in everyday life against whom one can fight. If there's a designated boogeyman, however, anger is easier to summon and focus. That's

30. *Cockfight.*

While the fighting was going on only a few miles away, cockfights with heavy betting were being held in Cholon.

the nice thing about war—it comes with distinct, easy-to-recognize bad guys to shoot, bomb, maim, and kill. Unfortunately, war also gives rise to enemies who are not necessarily distinct and easy to recognize—for example, supposedly "friendly" civilians who may be covertly abetting the enemy's efforts, or military allies with questionable allegiances and loyalty. The very existence of these enemies in disguise threatens our safety, and when we're threatened we get . . . angry.

Eyes Right! explores the anger that can smolder between those who are not necessarily enemies, yet are not quite friends. *Eyes Right!* is a scene laced with provocative sexual and sexist overtones, a graphic rendering of emotions as old as Eden and as sharp as the spike on a stiletto shoe. In his sketch, Gene shows us two American soldiers, both gigantic military police-types, as they pass a local Saigon lovely on the street. The first behemoth shoots what could be a slyly discreet—or, perhaps more likely, a suggestive and disrespectful—glance at the young local woman who seems determined

31. *Eyes Right!*

This street scene in Saigon features two American military policemen noticing a young Vietnamese woman as she passes them on the street. She wears a garment frequently seen in Vietnam, call an *áo dài*, which features tightly fitting pants with a long blouse over it, with the ends of the blouse slit for ease of movement.

to ignore them. We don't need to see her face to sense her anger at their uninvited leer. She is a mere object to these louts—an object obviously not worth their respect and one barely worth ogling—and we know that she knows what they're thinking. Lest there be any confusion on this point, the artist plants a look of angry indifference on the companion soldier as he receives the request for "eyes right." *Why? There's nothing over there worth looking at. I've seen enough skinny peasants for one lifetime.* It is, of course, a scene that could just as easily play in New York or Los Angeles as in Saigon. Disrespect and the anger it spawns aren't unique to war.

Hidden anger between uneasy noncombatants is even more obvious in *What a Deal!* The implications here are clear—the two soldiers feel cheated, and consequently, they are angry. But the accused merchant resents the implication that she's a cheater, so now she's angry, too.

As the typically sharp line between combatants and noncombatants begins to blur, the rationale for angry feelings on both sides paradoxically becomes clearer. Gene seizes on this premise in *Contraband Inspection* and *Junk Search*. According to him, "Most interceptions were done in a 'friendly' manner. If anything, interactions between the military and the locals tended to be indifferent." But not always.

These two scenes depict the tense Vietnam nautical encounters that sometimes occurred between civilians and military personnel. We assume that the military party crashers are, for better or worse, exactly what they appear to be—police-types trying to keep smugglers at bay. But who are these suspicious civilians? Are they noncombatants? Or are they "undeclared combatants" covertly helping the enemy by transporting contraband, guns, or worse? Because you can't distinguish friend from foe, everyone is presumed to be dangerous. Not surprisingly, the objects of suspicion react with anger and subdued hostility of their own. Is it any surprise that the Vietnamese woman in *Junk Search* poses defiantly with her cigar clenched tightly between her teeth?

Anger between combatants. Frank Moore Colby once observed, "I know of no more disagreeable sensation than to be left feeling generally angry without anybody in particular to be angry at."[5] To combat this feeling, one needs to find legitimate enemies upon which to unleash an inner pit bull—and not just the hapless road-rage-inducing

32. *What a Deal!*
"How dare you accuse my black market of dishonesty?"

33. *Contraband Inspection.*

The Coast Guard cutter *Point Welcome*, a vessel whose length I esti-mate to have been around ninety feet, dwarfs the tiny fishing boat whose passengers are being questioned by American soldiers. The cutter's seasick Vietnamese interpreter, shown in *Junk Search*, is belowdecks at this point.

denizens of the overcrowded highway, nor even the murky "may-be-they're-bad-guys-and-maybe-they're-not" noncombatants poten-tially lurking among the friendly citizenry. These foes need to be real enemies, the unequivocally evil kind you want to kill simply because . . . they need killing. More precisely, the kind of enemy Gene sets up in *Salvo over the 17th Parallel.*

But it turns out that killing the enemy is not as easy as it ought to be. As General William Tecumseh Sherman noted in 1865, "It is only those who have neither fired a shot nor heard the shrieks and groans of the wounded who cry aloud for blood, more vengeance,

BASSET
COAST GUARD
CUTTER
POINT WELCOME

34. *Junk Search.*

The Coast Guard cutter *Point Welcome* patrolled along the shoreline. With the assistance of a Vietnamese officer, who was seasick the whole time I was on board, the cutter would stop and inspect small junks. That officer served as a translator, and would come up on deck only when needed, remaining in agony below at other times. He is depicted holding a megaphone through which he speaks to the woman and her fellow passengers on the small fishing boat: "Ask her what brand she's smoking."

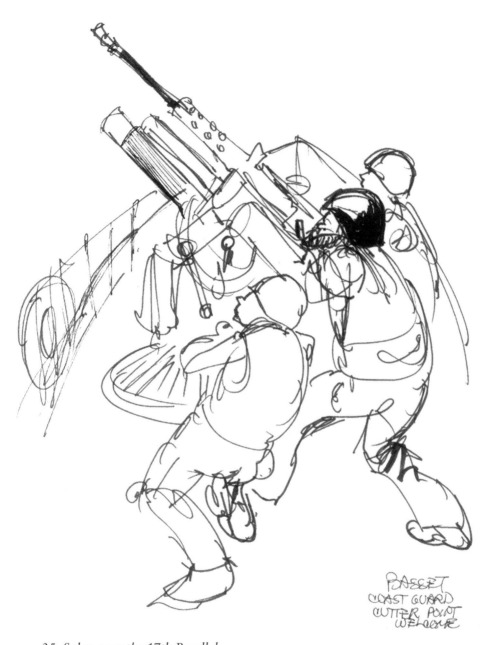

BASSET
COAST GUARD
CUTTER POINT
WELCOME

35. *Salvo over the 17th Parallel.*

The patrol of the *Point Welcome* up the coast from Da Nang to the 17th Parallel and back took three to four days, and this drawing was made near the northern limits of the vessel's journey. The captain instructed his crew to fire the large, fifty-caliber machine gun, not intending to hit anything, and the North Vietnamese responded shortly after with similarly ineffective fire, an exercise in mutual noise-making. A year later, friendly fire from U.S. aircraft killed two crew members.

more desolation."[6] What Gene shows us in *Salvo over the 17th Parallel* is a worthy alternative to slaughter, a way to express and/or work through anger without all the nastiness of actual combat. *Fire a few shells, make a lot noise, let off some steam.* As the artist implies, shooting guns ineffectively—but in the general direction of a specific, real enemy—is a fine way to vent anger without having to actually kill someone. None of us are strangers to this kind of behavior. We constantly engage in surrogate activities that allow us to direct anger at specific enemies without necessarily killing them. The Boston Red Sox might metaphorically want to kill the New York Yankees, but that would be somewhat problematic; instead they engage them in combat on the diamond several times every year.[7]

There are other ways to direct anger at an enemy without having to watch the ugly consequences (and feel the inevitable guilt) unfold. Why not hurl your anger from afar? Launching missiles and dropping bombs are two classic ways of unleashing hell upon an enemy without having to wash the grotesque consequences off your clothes or your retinas. As discussed earlier, nothing captures realism like a well-done photograph, and perhaps no picture shows the horror of war better than the famous 1972 Pulitzer Prize–winning photo taken by Nick Ut of nine-year-old Phan Thi Kim Phuc, shown burned and naked as she runs down the road after being accidentally struck with napalm during an air strike on Trang Bang conducted by "friendly" South Vietnamese forces.[8] No sane bomber pilot could do his job if he had to actually look at the fruits of his angry actions, no matter how infrequently scenes like this occur (although it's doubtful that they occur infrequently), nor how righteous the anger was that provoked the aggression.

Gene recognizes the idea of "I'm angry—and I'm going to do something about it—but I don't want to see the consequences of my actions" in *Clear for a Bombing Run up North*. Through his depiction of the highly choreographed aircraft carrier take-off ritual, the artist reminds us that the depersonalization of serious anger reaches farther than the hand that will push the button on the plane's instrument panel and drop those really big bombs on an enemy. The pilot may be the immediate agent of death, but the pirouetting marshaller who directs the takeoff is likewise throwing his own angry punch at an enemy he may never have to watch die. His boss, likely watching this scene from the nearby control tower, is doing the same. So is

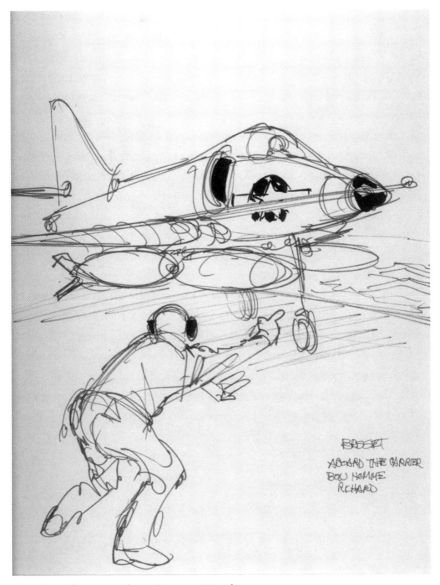

BASSET
ABOARD THE CARRIER
BON HOMME
RICHARD

36. *Clear for a Bombing Run up North.*

    I spent about four days aboard the aircraft carrier *Bon Homme Rich-ard*, stationed on the South China Sea. My flight there from Da Nang took about half an hour. Like many other war correspondents, I was mostly on my own and would arrange my excursions with the help of the public information officer of whichever base he was stationed, and this was how I found myself on the aircraft carrier. I also had the opportunity to fly on a bombing run, but did not do so. I recall that I never felt unwelcome by the soldiers on the various missions, who would likely have been instructed by the information officers to cooperate, possibly in order to make the war activities seem as positive as possible.

the commander of the ship. As is the two-star general in Saigon who developed this particular bombing strategy. And the four-star general in Washington who put his two-star compatriot in charge. And so forth. A lot of collective anger is about to lift off from this flattop and wreak havoc, but nobody is going to see the gory consequences of their anger up close.

And then there's the anger between combatants that produces the kind of dreadful consequences that you cannot fail to see, because they happen in front of you. Or around you. Or sometimes to you. This is the anger Gene shows us in *Fatal Fire Fight*.

Fatal Fire Fight is immediately different from any of the other drawings in this collection because it includes two versions of the same scene. Although Gene tried to sketch events as they were occurring, some events either moved too quickly, were not fully appreciated while they were still in progress, or were simply too dangerous to capture in real time. This is one of those events. The ambush bristles with anger, hostility, and danger—there's a soldier down and probably dead—and the viewer can practically feel enemy bullets whizzing past the artist's head. True to form, Gene creates an on-the-spot draft that captures the horror of combat as it takes place. The sketch

37. *Fatal Fire Fight, Version 1.*

is raw, but nevertheless conveys the emotions of sudden, unexpected, deadly battle reasonably well. But in this instance the preliminary drawing does not depict things quite the way Gene feels it should. The result is a second, more careful drawing made much later—after he'd had an opportunity to sort out, digest, and hone the details and emotions he could feel (but couldn't take the time to express with his pen and ink) while someone was shooting at him.

Anger at the side effects and circumstances of war. The story behind *Grab the Pigs before the Cows Get Loose* is pathetic, if only for the fact that it leaves us feeling sorry for the fate of farm animals at a time when the lives of young soldiers are in danger. Try to imagine the mindset of the men in the plane. They've survived the likes

38. *Fatal Fire Fight, Version 2.*

On patrol with Green Berets and a small company of Montagnards. We passed a group of fishermen in a fairly rushing stream. On our return, we were hit by fire from the opposite bank where the fishermen had been. I ducked behind a rock as the Montagnard in front of me was hit in the head and the Green Beret was hit in the legs. The Montagnards scattered and the return fire was by the Green Berets using a grenade launcher. My sketchbook took a bullet during the fight.

of snipers, punji sticks, and rocket attacks, but now it's possible they are all going to die simply because some rambunctious animals have busted loose inside the cargo plane and are raising such a ruckus that they may precipitate a crash. The viewer is likely to feel angry about this ridiculous situation. But angry at whom, exactly? There's no real enemy here (you surely can't count ill-mannered swine as an enemy) except for the war itself. The surreal, almost comical, opportunity to die that the war has created for the crew of this transport plane is Gene's reminder that war not only manufactures a million of its own unique opportunities to feel angry at your enemy, but it also comes equipped with the same incidental impediments to life, liberty, and the pursuit of happiness that irk us mercilessly in civilian life. General George S. Patton learned this lesson—the hard way—when he survived the brutal combat campaign across Europe only to die in a Jeep accident before making it back home. Not every war-related danger, it seems, involves an encounter with the enemy. According to Gene, war is associated with the same dangerous and anger-evoking situations we experience during peacetime. *If you're not dodging bullets on the battlefield you might be suffocating a planeload of rioting pigs to keep your plane from crashing.* It's apparent that war comes with side effects and bizarre circumstances that have little to do with war itself, but nonetheless drive us to anger.

Anger at "the enemy within." Walt Kelly died in 1973, two years before the fall of Saigon. Speaking through his widely syndicated comic strip *Pogo*, he once crafted a single line that has gained enormous fame as perhaps the best summary of the human condition ever written (at least the best line ever written by a "mere cartoonist"). As Kelly puts it, "We have met the enemy, and he is us." At no time is this sentiment more appropriate than during war. It seems that the enemy we place in our gunsight may not be the one who fills us with the most anger. Our greatest sources of anger, even during wartime, are often found among our partners, allies, and brethren.

Gene makes this connection in *A Woman's Work Is Never Done*. At first, the drawing seems a little cryptic. Why are these two Vietnamese women laboring while the apparently flirtatious Vietnamese soldier makes small talk? My initial interpretation was that this scene had nothing to do with anger and everything to do with the socially inept military pug who couldn't pick up a girl in a bar last night, so today he's trying to pick one up at the local construction sight. In

BASSET
ABOARD C123

⑩

39. *Grab the Pigs before the Cows Get Loose.*

Also onboard the C-123 transport that I took from Da Nang to the highlands base at Gia Vuc was a cargo of pigs and cows. Some of the pigs got loose, and their activity threatened to disturb the cows, which, if provoked, could have caused the plane to crash from a sudden shift of weight. We on board quickly stuffed the pigs into grain sacks, which suffocated them. At Gia Vuc, the Vietnamese would not eat the pork from those animals, and seeing a bad omen in the situation, I remember pork being served at the American base for the entire three weeks I was there.

Kübler-Ross terms, I couldn't figure out if this scene depicted denial (it will if she says no) or acceptance (if she says yes). When asked for more details (admittedly five decades later), Gene could not offer any meaningful clarification. It seems he didn't necessarily understand what he saw going on here. As he likes to say, "I just drew things as they happened."

However, the language-department interpreters at Mayo Clinic had no trouble pointing out what seems, in retrospect, obvious. Based upon the circumstances in the drawing and certain aspects of the women's attire, it turns out that these two laborers are most likely North-leaning prisoners who have been assigned to a labor detail. In the opinion of Mayo's Asian translators, these are two local Communist sympathizers (according to them, the hat on the woman holding the shovel is "the kind worn by Communists") who have been sentenced to a work detail for their "crimes." Rather than being the objects of a potentially lousy pick-up line, they are actually political prisoners guarded by a leering, abusive soldier. With this in mind, the anger becomes painfully apparent. The translators were quick to point out that women in this situation would frequently be beaten by a guard like this one. Or worse. So the prisoners hate the guard. And the guard hates the prisoners. The only real question here is, "Between prisoners and guard, who harbors the most anger?"

The scene that arguably addresses anger best—even if it's not exactly the type of anger that Kübler-Ross describes as a necessary step in the resolution of the grieving response to war—is *You #%@*! Next Time Don't Forget the #*!@ Beer.* Gene felt the fist-shaking Green Beret "summed up the war experience well: the routine killing of the enemy, the routine of shooting rats with a crossbow, training the Montagnards, the waiting . . . and no beer."

The artist is spot-on with his observation and analysis here. War, Gene suggests, gives rise to all sorts of anger. Rational forms of anger, especially those directed at dangerous and obvious enemies are easy to understand: My enemy wants to kill me. I want to kill him. Less dramatic, but just as easily understood, is the anger directed at Vietnamese civilians, traffic, animals, and a huge assortment of noncombatants. This scene depicts anger of a different type—anger directed at a nameless, faceless bureaucracy composed of friends and allies—anger that cannot be justified at this place and time but exists simply because the offended individual is angry

40. *A Woman's Work Is Never Done.*

During the conflict in Vietnam, many women were involved in projects requiring hard physical labor. In this image, two women haul materials using their hands and a barrow as a Vietnamese soldier watches.

about the war. In this case, the failure of a buddy to remember to bring beer triggers a soldier's wrath.

In another place and time, when the grief of war wasn't messing with brain cells, this type of transgression would be something to laugh about. But in this setting it's as painful as cancer. That's what war does to you. First, you deny. Then you get angry. But anger isn't always righteous. Sometimes you're angry because you didn't get your beer.

41. *You #%@*! Next Time Don't Forget the #*!@ Beer.*

I could sympathize at the rage and disappointment of this Green Beret, who continues to berate the crew of the supply plane even after the craft has taken off, for forgetting to bring a supply of beer.

Anger at the airlines. Anyone who flies on a regular basis is painfully aware of the unique, mind-numbing, ever-present anger that accompanies modern commercial air travel. High prices, delays, canceled flights, bad food (if any at all), over-bookings, unsympathetic employees, luggage fees—and rarely a believable, timely explanation

42. *Standby Passengers.*

    A mixed-rank group of military personnel wait in line at the military airport in Saigon, near the flight check-in location, to see if there might be room on board for them after all.

for anything that goes wrong. For many, air travel has become one of the most predictably frustrating and anger-evoking activities in which they participate.

The same foibles of flying were apparently an issue in 1965 as well because Gene captures the angry mood perfectly in *Standby Passengers*. Think about it: These people are going home. They're still alive and healthy. They ought to be happy. But they're not. Humans are an odd species. They get sent to 'Nam and survive shootings, bombs, diseases, and myriad other serious and potentially lethal injuries, yet they still get angry at the airport because of a few delays and distractions. Why? Are humans that irrational? The answer, of course, is yes.

Benjamin Franklin once said, "Anger is never without a reason, but seldom with a good one."[9] But I'm guessing he never flew through O'Hare.

3

Bargaining

We learn to bargain at an early age. "Eat your vegetables," our parents tell us. "Or what?" we ask bravely—albeit in a tiny, cautiously muted voice too soft for parental ears to hear. It seems that even children understand that it can be dangerous to bargain too aggressively with someone who has the ability to send you to bed without dinner. The mere fact that it's nutritionally in our best interest to eat those veggies doesn't mean we can't hold out for a better deal. "If I eat the carrots, then can I have chocolate sauce on my dessert?"

Kids bargain over a lot more than dessert, of course. In *First Aid*, a young child receives treatment from a military doctor for a minor injury, and anyone who's ever taken their offspring to the doctor appreciates that some serious bargaining is taking place behind the scene. If little Jimmy back in Columbus isn't going to sit still for his tetanus shot, what makes us think little Ngoc in Gia Vuc is going to behave while the doctor pulls a shard of sharp steel out of her leg? Gene Basset understands the intense negotiations in progress here; although he depicts everyone in the scene, child included, as paragons of calmness and patience, the tranquility on display likely means that the torrent of unseen threats and bribery that were surely unleashed in the preceding moments are still working their magic. The scene makes us smile, partly because there's such a sweet, trusting expression on the child's face, but also because we can't help but find it amusing that three seemingly competent adults have been forced to bargain with a two year old. Less charming is the idea that little Ngoc already recognizes she can compel three adults to bargain with her.

Under normal circumstances, people spend a great deal of their lives bargaining for various things, and in the perpetual grief of war-ravaged Vietnam it should surprise no one that bargaining—the third stage of Kübler-Ross' response to grief—seems prevalent.

43. *First Aid.*
    Medic Sergeant Bircher tends to the minor injury of a small child, whose mother looks on. Bircher is assisted by a Vietnamese woman with medical training, who also could serve as an interpreter.

Shouldn't we expect to see numerous bargaining-related scenes in Gene's collection? The answer is yes. And Gene, as expected, delivers.

Bargaining is the process through which parties agree to give up something of value in exchange for the fulfillment of certain pre-determined obligations. The Kübler-Ross concept of bargaining is relatively straightforward: the grieving subject hopes that a tragic loss can somehow be reversed through bargaining, and thus he or she negotiates desperately with some Supreme Being in a metaphysical version of "Let's Make a Deal." *Dear God, just bring back little Fido and I promise I'll adopt all the homeless puppies in Bolivia.* But as a psychological maneuver, bargaining is a short-lived and inevitably unsuccessful strategy. God, it turns out, does not negotiate with the likes of us. The direct-to-deity approach to bargaining is also a difficult, if not impossible, activity to observe, and is equally difficult to capture with ink and paper. Fortunately, there are other situations in which the act of bargaining is not only more productive but also more picturesque; the depiction of these situations can serve as surrogates for abstract examples of grief-driven bargaining. Gene surely witnessed people bargaining with one another all across Vietnam, and perhaps these scenes heightened a previously unrecognized sensitivity to the subtle connection that war creates between bargaining and grieving. If so, this could explain why so many of Gene's Vietnam sketches are set in local marketplaces.

According to Milton Friedman, "The most important single central fact about a free market is that no exchange takes place unless both parties benefit."[1] This truth does not, of course, preclude the distinct possibility that one party might benefit from the deal a little more than the other; it seems that you don't necessarily get what's fair out of life—you get that for which you negotiate.[2] In *Farmers' Market*, Gene conducts a tour through the local University of Bargaining. These folks, like the woman in the center of the sketch, may seem like "simple" farmers when they're toiling in the fields, but once they squat down in the Asian agora they magically become professors of commodity trading. In the open-air marketplaces of Vietnam, the fine art of bargaining is learned, perfected, and practiced with no less intensity than one finds in the trading pits of New York. Gene might find it difficult to draw grieving war victims negotiating with God, but he can show us how some of these same victims negotiate with customers.

The free market represents the real-world epitome of bargaining—"And after all," we ask, "isn't the preservation of a free market the reason for fighting these godless northern Communists in the first place?" But what happens when the free market isn't really free? What if unwieldy regulations and bungling bureaucracy clog the cogs that turn the great Vietnamese bargaining machine? Answer: free markets cease to exist. Yet even without a free market, people will continue to bargain with one another. Nature abhors a free-market vacuum, and she will inevitably create something to fill the void. Gene shows us her alternative solution in *Black Market—Only Place to Get Steel-Soled*

44. *Farmers' Market*.
    The daily open market in Da Nang was bustling and featured fresh fish and produce.

Shoes. Citing Milton Friedman once again, the economist points out that "black market was a way of getting around government controls. It was a way of enabling the free market to work. It was a way of opening up, enabling people." Indeed, in Vietnam the black market was, in most cases, the real free market. Gene initially found the scope of black-market activities overwhelming. "For example, there was a Chinese fellow who ran a black market in Jeeps. This was a serious enterprise. Anybody—even the U.S. military—who wanted a Jeep on short notice found themselves dealing with him. There was even a waiting list! Obviously he had a source of incoming supplies from a civilian contractor—or maybe the military itself. Like in Iraq or Afghanistan, graft is part of waging war. The black market is universal. That seemed really unusual to me at first, but not so much later on."

Black Market is one of the most powerful images in Gene's collection. The artist doesn't show us the usual Kübler-Ross "negotiations with God" aimed at getting back something that has already been taken away—no, this is an upfront bargain with the devil, and it's meant to keep something from being lost in the first place. The angst on the soldier's face conveys his thoughts with clarity: *Okay God . . . if I buy these expensive boots, you won't let sharp bamboo sticks punch through my feet*. But what price is he willing to pay for the intangible extra margin of safety that might accompany this purchase? The cost of a carton of cigarettes? His soul? Based upon the sergeant's pained and conflicted facial expression, the answer is, "You know, God, you're asking a lot for these boots. Are they really worth it?" In a single scene Gene thus cleverly confronts us with a crucial question about "bargaining" in Vietnam (or any other war): if this soldier is unsure that the benefits provided to him by steel-soled boots are worth the price, how can we expect a nation to decide whether the benefits of war are ultimately worth the price?

The traditional markets (open or black) may be the place where one bargains for fresh fish, produce, or steel-soled boots, but there's a whole lot of bargaining going on in other settings. Negotiations have taken place over the entirety of human history, and one type of bargaining in particular has been practiced for so long that it's generally recognized as the basis for the world's oldest profession: prostitution. Gene tells us that "there was actually very little contact between the military and the populace. Except, of course, when sex was available." According to him, "sex in war gives a lot of young

45. *Black Market—Only Place to Get Steel-Soled Shoes.*

When I first arrived in Saigon, I wandered into an area called Cholon, where the black market was much in evidence. I sketched this image of an American soldier buying a pair of combat boots with steel-plated soles, which served to protect against punji sticks. These were sharpened bamboo sticks placed by the enemy randomly in fields where the soldiers might walk. They were coated with animal dung or other foul substances and would penetrate through the soles of regular-issue boots into soldiers' feet, often causing deadly infection. The official supply of the more protective boots was still insufficient, and servicemen would turn to the black market for protection.

GIs the exposure and freedom they didn't have at home—and it's cheap. The local women are Asians, so it lends a certain exoticism to the mix. And we know that sex in politics is about power, so that might be another part of involvement."

Given Gene's (subconscious) focus on bargaining, his fascination with soldiers at war, and his keen appreciation of human nature, we'd be frankly shocked if the sex trade escaped without depiction. Once again, the artist does not disappoint. Gene provides not one, not two, but three sketches detailing interactions between soldiers and sex workers during the war.

In *Nice Dirty Pictures*, Gene reminds us of a basic truth about bargaining—it doesn't happen unless both parties are interested in the transaction. In this case, the soldier's face tells the viewer that he's indifferent to the young man's explicit goods (which may be, as Gene suggests in the caption, simple pornography; or it might be photos of girls he can make available for a price). The prostitute loitering up the street is just as likely to be scorned for her efforts. The lesson is a good one—sometimes the customer wants a little companionship and affection, and sometimes he just wants steel-soled shoes. If you have something the customer wants, great. But if there's no buyer interest in the item for sale, there won't be any bargaining for it.

It's appropriate that Gene explores the idea that "there are certain things for which you cannot bargain" in *Nice Dirty Pictures*, because the specific type of bargaining described by Kübler-Ross falls directly into this category—the third stage of grieving is really non-bargaining rather than bargaining because the desired outcome (i.e., undoing the loss or harm) is not something for which one can actually negotiate. On the other hand, the baby-faced GI in *Nice Girl* is definitely interested in pursuing the bargaining process a bit more extensively. Between the soldier's intense gaze, the pimp's well-polished laugh-a-minute sales pitch, and the policeman's obvious and deliberate disregard for the events going on, one knows with near certainty that there is something more being served inside this abode than "real American food." We get a teasing glimpse of these indoor activities in *R and R on Thudo Street*, a scene quite possibly drawn on the other side of the same door through which the parade is passing in *Nice Girl*. *R and R on Thudo Street* depicts a story as old as love itself: boy meets girl, boy bargains with girl, boy pays girl, boy loses girl, etc. And the economy marches on.

46. *Nice Dirty Pictures.*

The GI is offered pornography, while a bit further up the street a prostitute looks on expectantly, wondering if the soldier might want what she has to offer instead of—or in addition to—the photos being presented.

47. *Nice Girl.*

A GI on bar-lined Thudo Street is being introduced to a prostitute, who leads him into a building for a tryst. This image was published in U.S. newspapers under the bowdlerized caption "Come, Real American Food."

48. *R and R on Thudo Street*.
    Thudo Street was a well-known red light district in Saigon, featuring bars that were frequented by prostitutes.

Moving back into the world of G-rated scenes, Gene acknowledges that not all bargains involve overt, visible grief, even when grief is surely present in every aspect of the subject's life (and not all bargains involving personal service are pornographic in nature—sometimes a job is just a job). In *Shoeshine Lady*, a young Vietnamese woman fulfills her end of a bargain by polishing the combat boots of a sleeping soldier. There's no explicit grief (or sex) here; scenes depicting stereotypical happy-go-lucky shoeshine artists at work have graced countless hotel lobbies, rattling Amtrak sleeper cars, and practically every black-and-white gangster movie ever made. If not for Gene's written reminder that she is working "for a pittance," we might miss the loss and, with it, the grief lurking just below the surface of the sketch.

49. *Shoeshine Lady.*

Many of the U.S. soldiers would hire local people to do a number of personal tasks, usually for a pittance, and this often included shining boots.

The need to bargain is not, of course, exclusive to the underclass or those who must work "for a pittance." Rank, social or otherwise, does not insulate you from bargaining. Gene assures us of this in *Sir, You're Overweight*. Here, a colonel comes face-to-face with cold reality; despite his senior stature within the military pecking order, he must nonetheless negotiate—just like the lowly private standing in line behind him—to get his overweight baggage out of the country. Gene surely must have taken some small degree of pleasure in seeing these negotiations occurring without regard to rank (although the obviously impatient private would likely prefer it if this particular bargaining session was not slowing the line in front of him). Finishing off his commentary on the complex relationship between social status and bargaining, the artist apparently cannot resist adding a follow-up sketch, *(Untitled)*, depicting a spontaneous outbreak of "collective bargaining" by the GI underclass.

COLONEL SIR,... YOU'RE OVERWEIGHT

50. *Sir, You're Overweight.*

American military personnel typically flew into Saigon first and from the Tan Son Nhut airport they would fly out to other locations. In this drawing, a colonel waits at the head of the line, in front of a private, only to find that his luggage is over the weight limit. The operation was thus handled in a manner similar to commercial airlines, often without regard for rank.

51. *Untitled.*

1965 was the start of the massive buildup of the war. The standby lines for crowded troop carriers were also building up.

The good bargainer negotiates for a clearly defined goal. The better bargainer negotiates for a disguised goal, while appearing to bargain for something else—that is, he bargains with an ulterior motive. Gene witnessed countless acts of bargaining over hidden agendas in Vietnam. In *Tactical Planning*, the Vietnamese river patrollers are negotiating their assignments for the day. They're ostensibly discussing how to arrange the best matchups: boat-type versus enemy capability, patrol routes versus known Viet Cong positions, firepower versus enemy defensive capabilities, and the like. Or at least that's what they seem to be negotiating. In reality, everyone is simply bargaining for an assignment in which they are unlikely to encounter the enemy. As Gene suggests in the caption, what they seem to be negotiating isn't what they're really negotiating.

Negotiations with a hidden agenda aren't the only acts of deceptive bargaining one routinely encounters. There are many others, but none more intellectually dishonest than the act of bargaining when, in reality, one (or sometimes both) parties have no intention of actually negotiating anything. They simply want to look like they're bargaining. Governments in particular do this a lot. Gene laughs at

52. *Tactical Planning.*
The Americans running the military base at Junk Base II would attempt to plan the direction and duration of the patrols. Such efforts, the goal of which was to locate the enemy, were sometimes thwarted when the mostly Vietnamese soldiers sought ways to avoid contact with the enemy rather than seeking them out.

this type of charade in *Here's the Plan*. The artist shows us a Green Beret officer who expects his Vietnamese charges to obey his instructions. But clearly the troops have a different idea. Gene remembers that "I saw many cases where Americans were disillusioned by the Vietnamese. For example, I often heard about the limited combat values of certain local soldiers. The Montagnards were notorious for running from firefights. The cause for the war, at least in this case, apparently had no value to the hill tribe." The artist leaves it to the viewer to complete the scene. What are the soldiers' unspoken terms for participation in the officer's master plan? Does the officer even recognize that negotiations are occurring here? Who will ultimately give up and give in?

We may choose to bargain directly with others, or—when things get really uncomfortable—we may try to foist the responsibility for bargaining off on someone else. Sometimes we pay a surrogate (like

53. *Here's the Plan.*
    The morning ritual of gathering a ragtag unit of Montagnards for a patrol outside Gia Vuc.

54. *Tell Him to Get Out before We Torch the Place.*

This was drawn on the patrol in which we were ambushed. A village that had been used by the Viet Cong as a base was burned in retaliation for the attack, and in this image a Montagnard soldier tells another to warn the inhabitant of the building in the background that he is in danger. The torching of the village resulted in the death of a handicapped child who was not able to get out in time. The potbellied pigs, one of which is seen in the drawing, presumably ran away and survived. The burning of villages was big news on U.S. television.

a lawyer) to do the bargaining for us, but sometimes we just flat-out dump the problem in someone else's lap. In *Tell Him to Get Out before We Torch the Place*, Gene shows a well-intentioned but overly busy Montagnard passing the buck on critical negotiations regarding a handicapped villager. In this case, the soldier turns over the responsibility for bargaining a safe escape for the handicapped villager to someone who presumably has a vested interest in seeing the young man survive. Unfortunately, according to Gene, the negotiations for "getting him out" ultimately failed and the young man perished in the flames. By delegating the responsibility for negotiations to another, the soldier affords himself a degree of plausible deniability for the tragic outcome.

55. *Roll Them Ivories.*

Gambling among the Vietnamese was quite common, as shown in this drawing of a dice game, which also depicts the unloading of a vessel in the background. This drawing was published with the caption "This is Not a Floating Crap Game—It's a Bargain Counter in Fish."

Gene concludes his observations on bargaining with *Roll Them Ivories*. Gambling, Gene observes, may be the purest and yet most complex form of bargaining possible. At one level, gambling is nothing more than a simple bargain: *I'll pay you if I lose. You'll pay me if I win.* But at another level, gambling requires that each player bargain with some higher power for the desired outcome: *just let me throw one more seven and I'll never miss church again.* Maybe it's not exactly the kind of grief-driven bargaining described by Kübler-Ross, but for the guy who's about to lose his family's income for the month, the bargaining is no less sincere.

4

Depression

According to Kübler-Ross, there will come a time when those who are working through the grieving process must also experience depression. Gene's Vietnam drawings support her prediction. Through the artist's hand we witness war-induced grief giving rise to a taint of depression from which no one—soldier or civilian, young or old—escapes untouched.

Gene eases into an examination of grief's fourth stage with *Going My Way* and *A Better 'Ole*. The two drawings remind us that depression doesn't always feel depressing. Comedians find humor in scenes of depression; indeed, it can be argued (based upon Twain's view that "humor is tragedy plus time")[1] that humorous things evolve over time from events rooted in post-traumatic grief and depression. In contrast, psychiatrists—and, it seems, our artist—find depression in humor. That makes sense. If, as the saying goes, we can "laugh on the outside while crying on the inside," it follows that seemingly humorous experiences might be dissected for subtle elements of depression.

Going and *Better 'Ole* aren't depressing at first glance. Gene initially makes us smile at the sights of a GI standing next to a sarcastically pointless sign—*as if anybody really cares that the San Diego Freeway is 11,800 miles away*—or a soldier trying to dig a six-foot-deep hole in a bowl of mud. There's subtle humor here. But on closer inspection we see the emotional darkness lurking in plain sight. The men Gene shows us are lonely, far from home, uncomfortable, exhausted, and seriously annoyed with their current predicaments. Lest there be any question as to whether these scenes are meant to conjure feelings of depression in the viewer's mind, Gene pulls the cartoonist's rabbit—a cold, relentless, gloomy and hopelessly cliché rain—out of his hat and uses it to make these already miserable situations just a little bit more depressing.

56. *Going My Way.*

The monsoon season brought much rain while I was in Vietnam, and I witnessed this incident in Da Nang in which a soaked American soldier is asking another for a ride. The makeshift sign indicating the mileage to San Diego was placed there by an unknown soldier as a reminder to his fellow service people of how foreign (and how far) the place was from home.

57. A Better 'Ole.

    I witnessed this scene featuring two American marines and was reminded of a famous wartime drawing by the British cartoonist Bruce Bairnsfather (1887–1959). Drawn during World War I, he had two Tommys in a muddy hole with shells whizzing around; one was grumbling and the other advised, "if you know of a better 'ole, go to it."

There are countless images of Vietnam that evoke depression in the viewer, but one in particular seems to capture Gene's attention: the soldier heading into battle. The artist sees fit to provide no less than four depression-themed images based on this scenario. The first three are portraits of overtly depressed soldiers quietly dealing with their own dark thoughts as they trek toward combat. In contrast, the men in the fourth scene don't project a sense of depression as they head off into harm's way; instead, this drawing invites the viewer to become depressed on their behalf.

Third Class Seating and *Scenic View of the War Front* explore the silent depression permeating the cramped fuselage of a turboprop as it cruises at 5,000 feet. *Third Class* is, without too much exaggeration, a flying hell. The plane is overcrowded, most certainly hot, possibly dangerous, fetid, uncomfortable, boring, and worst of all it provides its occupants with the perfect opportunity to reflect on everything that's gone wrong in the past and might go wrong in the future. The scene is so cluttered and muddled that foreground and background objects blur into unrecognizable doodles; the only things that stand out with clarity are the depressed faces. The situation is different in *Scenic View*, where the funk doesn't originate with the ruminations of the passengers but instead arises as a reflex response to scenes of destruction and ruin passing below the window. We don't have to see the faces of the men surveying the war-devastated countryside to feel their depression, nor do we need to actually see for ourselves what they are staring at; like a well-directed horror film, Gene's drawing lets the viewer imagine things outside these windows that are far worse than anything he can draw.

Just as rain evokes a sense of depression, so does darkness—except darkness can be even more depressing. Like the opening lines of "Invictus," by William Ernest Henley,[2] "Out of the night that covers me, Black as the pit from pole to pole . . ." Gene uses the blackness of night to convey a sense of depression. *Night Patrol*—conceptually one of the best sketches in the collection—depicts a boat crew trying to draw fire from unseen enemies hidden along the shore. We cannot distinguish the faces of the men—indeed, we can barely identify them as men at all. There are no physical details to appreciate. No conversation. No action. All we see are vague, silent, still shadows. And yet we can feel the sailors' depression as surely as we can feel our own pulses.

58. *Third Class Seating.*

This is a view inside a C-123 transport, a two-engine craft that, along with the larger, four-engine C-130, was one of the workhorses for the U.S. military in Vietnam. Such transportation was without frills, and little differentiation was made for rank of passenger.

Amazingly, the next drawing might be even better; Gene has told me that it's his favorite sketch from Vietnam. *Elephant Grass, Punji Sticks, Mines, and Viet Cong* shows three faceless, barely visible, soldiers heading off through the tall grass on patrol. The viewer is forced to ask uncomfortable questions: Will they return safely? Will there be injuries? Death? If they don't return, will they be missed? Who will miss them? Why are they doing this? Will anything they do out there make a difference five hundred years from now? The soldiers are too focused on their mission to dwell on these questions. Or feel depressed. The viewer, on the other hand, cannot help but

59. *Scenic View of the War Front.*

This drawing was made on board the C-123 transport that brought me from Saigon to Da Nang. The soldiers look out over the landscape, and their view likely included large empty areas where napalm had burned away the trees or where the defoliant Agent Orange had been used.

ask these questions—and become depressed as they mull over the rhetorical answers.

War produces casualties. In *Waiting for Chopper . . . One Dead, One Wounded*, Gene shows us human carnage as he relates the tale of his own harrowing brush with peril. He has confronted us with casualties before; we saw fallen soldiers in the combat scenes of chapter 2. But this scene feels distinctly different from those presented earlier. Now we've evolved to a more advanced Kübler-Ross stage of grief. In the heat of battle, the predominant grief reaction was anger. Once the fighting ends, the emotional responses change. Anger abates. Depression sets in. That's what we're feeling here—depression. And Gene doesn't need to point out the obvious: the longer we're forced to wait for that helicopter, the more depressed we're going to become.

60. *Night Patrol.*

A nighttime scene, the shading on this drawing—which provides its nocturnal quality—was added after I disembarked from the patrol boat. The South Vietnamese flag flies at the head of the vessel, which made runs up and down the river, for the purpose of drawing fire from the enemy in order to make them reveal their locations.

Children aren't supposed to have health problems—they're just kids, right? It's not fair, it's not moral, and the thought of it is unsettling to most. Gene knows that we are soft touches for a puny, puking child, and he exploits our weakness to evoke feelings of depression. *Prenatal Instructions* and *Preventive Medicine* depict tired,

61. *Elephant Grass, Punji Sticks, Mines, and Viet Cong.*

Drawn while on patrol with the Green Berets in the region around Gia Vuc. The title indicates the danger of the relatively sparse locale. Elephant grass made it impossible to see the enemy; further dangers were at foot from land mines and the punji sticks that could pierce a soldier's foot right through his boot and cause infection from the animal dung and other septic materials with which the sticks were coated.

depressed mothers with their sick children. There's nothing particularly war-oriented about these scenes—if we change the clothes and the setting, they could just as easily be weary moms and cranky tots visiting the doctor's office in Kokomo, Indiana. It seems the links between ailing child and parental feelings of depression are similar in every culture. In *OB Sub Delivering by the Book*, the laboring mother and her soon-to-be-delivered offspring evoke the same emotions—this time from a nervously hovering and obviously worried father—as do the sick children portrayed in the previous sketches.

62. *Waiting for Chopper . . . One Dead, One Wounded.*

This drawing records the fatal ambush on the Green Beret patrol I accompanied on October 12, 1965. The fishermen they'd seen moments earlier turned out to be Viet Cong, and when the group was fired upon, I saw the head of the Montagnard in front of him partially blown off. That soldier lies close to death at the left of the drawing, while the American Green Beret medic, Sergeant Norman Bircher of Topeka, Kansas, who was behind me and whose legs were both severely wounded by the exploding bullets used by the enemy, is being carried off in a stretcher. I dove behind a rock and managed to escape serious injury, although one of my sketchbooks bears a bullet hole from the attack. A "Daily News Summary" issued on October 13 by the information office of the 6252nd Fighter Wing of the U.S. Air Force stated that the "patrol suffered moderate casualties."

63. *Prenatal Instructions.*

Green Beret medic Sergeant Norman Bircher, with his Vietnamese assistant's aid in translating, gives two tired-looking, expectant Vietnamese women, one of whom already has a young child she carries in her arms, instructions for good prenatal health. The weary mothers-to-be, perhaps feeling the information is being thrust upon them, seem less than enthusiastic about the encounter.

64. *Preventive Medicine.*
In Gia Vuc, one of the benefits of the presence of the Green Berets was that they offered medical aid to the inhabitants. For some, this was a first-time offer that was viewed with some trepidation and distrust.

Depression is a cunning foe. She may come to us in disguise. In *Saigon Landscape* and *Schoolhouse*, we encounter depression masquerading as boredom. The expression on the face of the central figure in *Landscape*, or the sleepy look of the little girl (located next to Gene's signature) in *Schoolhouse*, remind us that boredom and depression can appear—to an observer—identical.

In small doses, boredom is benign. Short periods of it are probably a good thing—boredom gives us the time and impetus to examine our lives, create goals, and store up the psychic energy needed

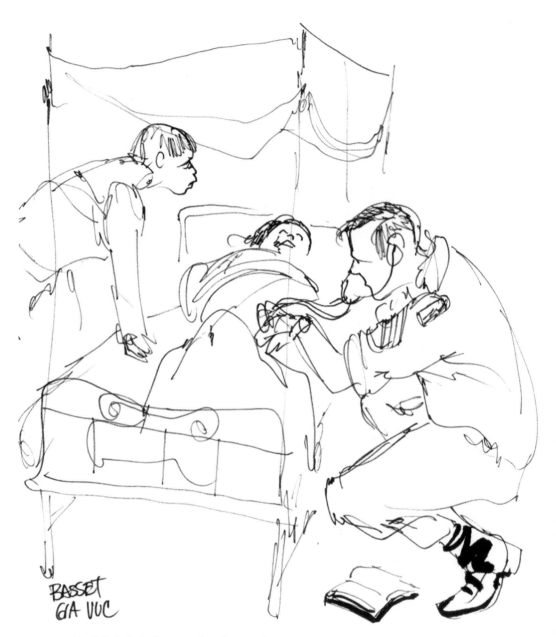

65. *OB Sub Delivering by the Book.*

   After medic Sergeant Bircher was wounded on patrol, another medic was brought in to the base in Gia Vuc. As an anxious father watches, the new medic, inexperienced in births, follows a medical guidebook to assist him in delivering the baby. I recall that the medical assistance offered by military personnel, especially in situations where there were complications, was generally accepted with gratitude by those who benefited from it.

66. *Saigon Landscape*.

    This cityscape contrasts the relative serenity of the old Catholic cathedral in Saigon with the hustle and bustle of the wartime city.

67. Schoolhouse.

In this drawing, a Vietnamese soldier teaches a disparate group of students in a classroom as another child—too young yet for school—looks wistfully through the window. Also visible in the background, seen through the open door, is a water buffalo.

to accomplish great things. But in large quantities, "boredom feeds depression."[3] Gene gets the idea that boredom and depression typically coexist, and in these drawings he swirls and mixes these two emotions together into a single psychologically dark cocktail.

Gene once again finds himself in a situation where it is not clear whether the predominant sentiment is depression or mere boredom. *Village Scene* takes us to a place where the war has turned a boring life into a depressed life. The people here appear to be drained of both energy and emotion. *What are they planning to do next? Indeed, are they planning to do anything at all?* Is this (i.e., sitting on the front porch watching the nearby jungle grow) as good as it gets? Even the pig seems either bored or depressed.

68. *Village Scene.*

This is one of several village scenes drawn while on patrol, and it, like others, includes the frequently present potbellied pig of Vietnam.

There is, however, no question about the emotion at play in the final set of drawings. *Starvation isn't boring, and there's nothing boring about scrounging for food.* This is depression at its prime.

Pay Day . . . in Salt might not be as depressing as it initially seems. These people are, after all, lined up to receive a "wage" for the work they've done. That's a good thing, and taken in proper context it's a positive—maybe even uplifting—image. But a gnawing sense of depression creeps in when we notice the broader picture. These are poor people eking out a living in wartime. There are women here. And children. And infants. They look poor and hopeless and defeated. And they're being paid in the most basic commodity one can imagine, something that, in Western culture, passes for worthless.

69. *Pay Day . . . in Salt.*

In the village of Gia Vuc, many workers were paid not in currency, but in salt, a valuable commodity in a locale where there was often no refrigeration. The workers line up in this drawing to receive their pay, and they include young children, one smoking as he waits for his wages, and a number of bare-breasted women. I recall that often U.S. FAC (Forward Air Control) pilots would land their fixed-wing small planes to pose with the women, as a memento.

Finally, there is a closing image. *Dig for Your Dinner* is, on so many levels, painful imagery. *Yes, we know that pain like this exists in the world, but it only occurs in places we never visit, and it only affects people we don't know. Right?* This is something we try not to think about—the idea of grownups and kids rooting through other people's trash for something to eat. But Gene makes us think about it, and suddenly it's not just the people in the picture who are depressed. Now we're depressed, too. This is the message the artist ultimately leaves with us—the idea that those who experience the grief of war firsthand aren't the only ones who need to deal with the resulting depression. Unfortunately, this type of depression is a communicable disease, and we're all at risk of catching it.

70. *Dig for Your Dinner.*

The refuse from the base camps in Da Nang included a great deal of still-edible food, and the local inhabitants would wait at the dump for the military trucks to arrive so they could salvage from their deposits. A soldier sweeps out the remains of the load from the back of the truck while the Vietnamese search for usable items, some of which might show up at the open market the following day.

5

Acceptance

This brings us to the final stage of our ink-on-paper tour through Vietnam, 1965: *acceptance*. It's not just the farthest, and therefore hardest-to-reach, destination on our trip. It's also the hardest to analyze. Just what is this thing that Kübler-Ross calls "acceptance"? What does it mean to "accept" an outcome?[1] Does acceptance require resolution of antecedent stages of grief? Maybe—it seems pretty obvious that you can't simultaneously be in denial about a grief-producing event while accepting that it has occurred. The same holds for bargaining—if you still think you can negotiate your way out of a situation, then you haven't accepted the finality of it. Perhaps you only need to resolve some of the stages of grief before you can accept the outcome? Like anger. Can you accept that something bad has happened and then move on even if you're still angry? Maybe. Ditto for depression—can you remain depressed about an outcome, yet still accept that it's happened? I suppose so, but it's surely a lot harder to move on with life when you're locked in the stocks of depression. Angry, endless rumination is probably not quite what Kübler-Ross had in mind when she wrote about acceptance.

No, Kübler-Ross's version of acceptance involves something more than the mere absence of denial, bargaining, anger, or depression. But what? How about surrender? Is "giving up the fight" necessary in order to accept an outcome? Of course, simply dropping your gloves and saying *"no mas"* falls woefully short of true acceptance. What about forgiveness? Can you ever really accept and move on without forgiving those responsible for your grief? What other forces could grease the transition from depression to acceptance? How about revenge? Does evening up the score help to resolve things? Does retribution? Or punishment? What if you simply "stop caring" about whatever it is that's causing your grief—does overwhelming ennui equate to an emotional acceptance of loss? It seems that all these possibilities, and many more, may, in some situations, be necessary to achieve acceptance, but by themselves neither constitute nor assure it. Acceptance—whether it's a psychological phenomenon, religious state, cosmic occurrence, or something else entirely—defies easy analysis.

Perhaps acceptance is best described functionally by its ultimate outcome—specifically, the ability to "move on" from grief and resume living. We may not understand the mechanics of acceptance as well as we understand simpler, more visceral responses like anger or depression, but we can tell when it has occurred by the actions that follow.

Passing Parade provides an optimistic look at acceptance and its potential to restore normality to the war-weary people of Vietnam. We see here a cross-section of humanity that includes, according to the artist, "soldiers, women, children, and Buddhist monks" all going on with their lives. These folks should be in the war-induced grips of denial, anger, and depression. But where are those negative emotions now? Like mail in the nearby post office, these people are slowly moving on, literally and figuratively, despite the war.

Acceptance is likewise a theme in *Street Scene*. Four characters—a couple on a motorbike, a child, and a policeman—represent extremes in the Vietnamese population, each of whom appears to have accepted for now the way things have turned out for them. War has surely given these figures reason to grieve, and as Basset suggests (in his reference to the future bombing that will occur right here) it's destined to cause grief again. These people likely realize that their suffering isn't over, but they've accepted it. And they're moving on.

If nothing works up an appetite like a busy day of denial, anger, bargaining, and depression, then nothing says, "I'm finally ready to accept things and move on" like a good meal. The next two drawings, *New Catches from the Sea* and *Roadside Diner*, make use of edible imagery. Basset lays out the whole food chain for us. Boats bring the food in, middlemen divide and distribute it, roadside chefs prepare it, and people eat it; we're an outhouse trip away from completing the proverbial circle of life. Inherent in Gene's culinary psychoanalysis is the tacit understanding that life goes on—and will continue to go on—despite the lumps of grief that war leaves in the gravy.

Complicated people lead complicated lives, and the cartoonist who wishes to explore them may need to make complicated drawings.

71. *Passing Parade.*

The main post office in Saigon was also the location of a number of important governmental and other offices. The crowd includes soldiers, women, children, and Buddhist monks.

It follows that a concept like acceptance might be easier for Gene to illustrate if he depicts subjects who live simple lifestyles. He takes this approach in *Village Scene* and *Native Quarters*. In these scenes the denizens of Gia Vuc show us what it looks like to accept the hard life, suffering, and grief imposed by war. Unfortunately, it looks a lot like the hard life they accepted before there was a war going on. Their life is boring. Repetitive. Not very intellectually stimulating—even the pot-bellied pigs seem tired of this jungle existence. The people appear to mutter to no one in particular, "Life in Vietnam . . . it is what it is." These villagers may have been served a bigger slice of grief pie than most of their countrymen, and yet they've still found ways to work through Kübler-Ross's stages. There's no denial here. No anger. No bargaining or depression. The only thing going on in Gia Vuc is life as usual. And in Gia Vuc, that life is dull.

72. *Street Scene.*

Another image of Saigon was this street scene of a soldier, a child, a couple on one of the ubiquitous mopeds, and a Citroën cab. In the background is the Hotel Caravelle, which was frequented by Americans and was the site of an explosion set off by the Viet Cong later in the conflict, before the Tet Offensive of 1968.

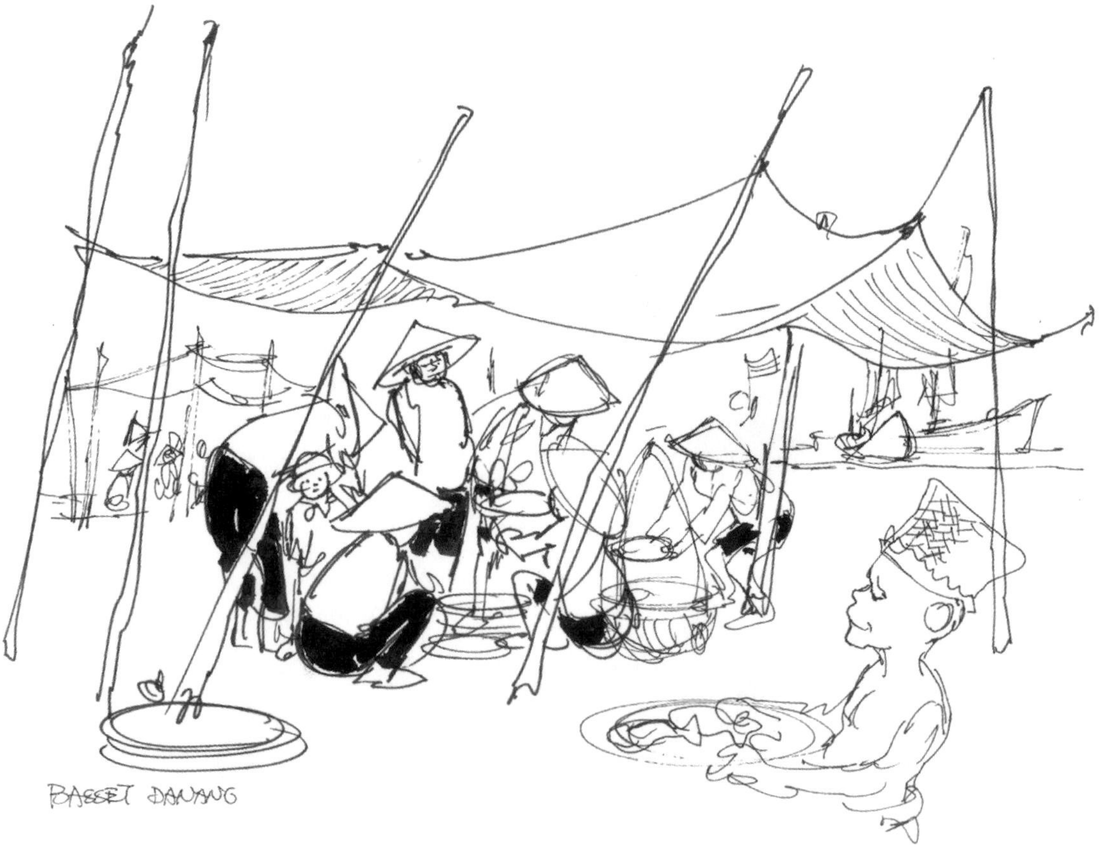
BASSET DANANG

73. *New Catches from the Sea.*

Drawn at the seaside in Da Nang, in the background, this image shows boats coming in with fish that will be sustenance for the city's citizens, while the Vietnamese consider what's available in the foreground. The U.S. base typically received its own supplies of food through different means.

But chronic boredom endows certain strengths upon those who suffer it. It's not hard to imagine how a lifetime of simple existence has helped these villagers to cope with certain emotional consequences of adversity and grief. Just look at *Breakdown*, in which a group of Gia Vucians has been stranded by a Jeep mishap. There is no anger or depression here. These folks aren't going to waste emotional energy getting upset or depressed over a small problem like a roadside stranding. They've been conditioned to jump straight to acceptance at times like this. And why not? After all, they're not going to be stuck here forever. This is an adventure. And, unlike so many other aspects of their lives, things related to this setback can only get better.

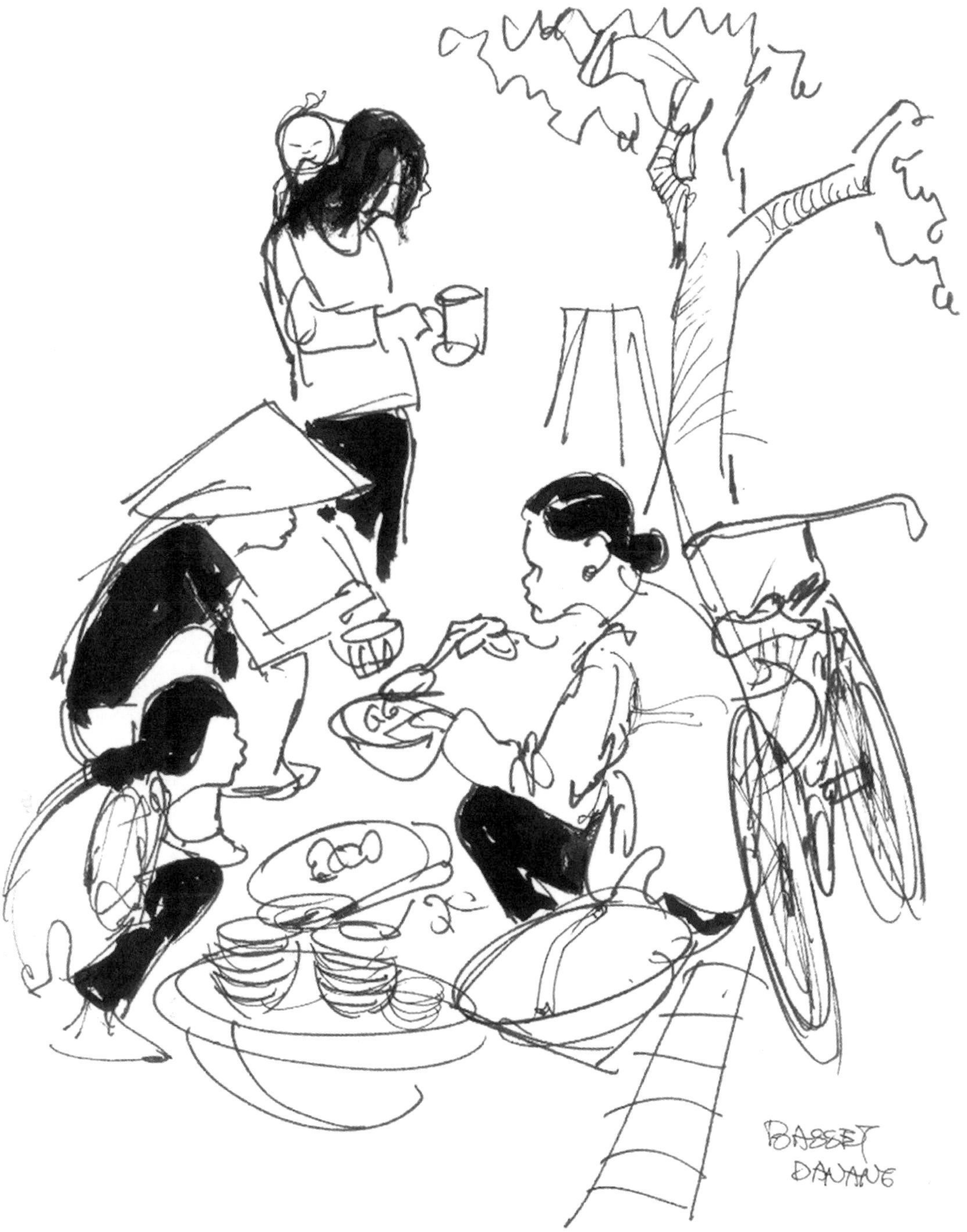

74. *Roadside Diner.*

Makeshift meal preparations and sales along the roadside, as shown in this drawing, were common in Da Nang. While some Americans were distrustful of the unregulated practice, and the principal patrons of such meals were Vietnamese, I sampled such offerings and found it to be a pleasurable experience.

75. *Village Scene.*

    This drawing shows some of the homes that were built up on stilts in and near the village of Gia Vuc. The rambling road in the right background leads up further into the highlands.

76. *Native Quarters.*

Most of the thatched homes in Gia Vuc were on a single level, but some were raised on stilts, which created space beneath that could be used as another level.

77. Breakdown.
    Some sort of mechanical failure and no one had any idea what to do about it.

Meanwhile, back in Da Nang, the Americans are into some serious acceptance of their own. No, the war isn't over—in fact, it's just getting geared up for the ugly seasons that will follow. But in *Inspection—All Set to Bomb*, it's clear that this American fighting man has accepted the war and is ready to move on. Even with his back to the viewer we can tell that the technician is satisfied with his work and content with the immediate plans to bomb—and perhaps kill—someone he's never met. Unlike Gene's previous drawings depicting men and their deadly flying machines (sketches that loosely suggest the denial, anger, etc., evoked by war), this scene is direct in its sentiment: *I've done my job.*

Acceptance, of course, doesn't mean "at peace." Merely accepting the finality of an outcome won't necessarily prevent a lifestyle from being hectic. The artist reminds us of this in *Tight Squeeze* and

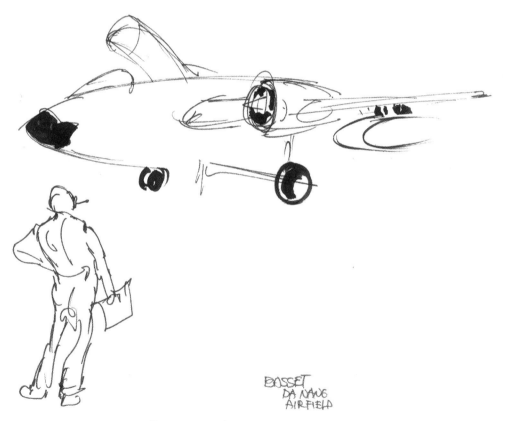

78. *Inspection—All Set to Bomb*.
A mechanic gives his final okay.

BASSET
DANANG HARBOR

79. Tight Squeeze.

The harbor at Da Nang is deep and very good, and it was often crowded with vessels varying widely in size, from the warship shown in the background of this drawing, to the rowboat and the junk in the lower right corner.

Traffic Jam where "normal" means chaotic, overcrowded, and confused. Gene is no sentimental fool; he knows better than to equate the peace that follows acceptance with the sappy peace of a Maxfield Parrish pastoral painting. Acceptance can be as disorganized and claustrophobic as any other stage of grief resolution, and you just have to deal with it.

Of course, pastoral scenes can provide fine visual metaphors for the idea of acceptance, as Gene reminds us in *Progress in the Highlands*, *Stuck in the Highlands*, and *Commuting Back to the Village*. Basset sees life carrying on for the people of Gia Vuc. But this life

80. *Traffic Jam*.

In Da Nang, every day was, in effect, moving day, since the inhabitants would typically pack up most of their belongings and take them along, even on trips short in distance and duration. They would pile themselves and their things into the French vehicles, which were often owned by some racketeer who charged plenty for the transportation. Traffic scenes were thus frequently very chaotic, with overloaded vehicles vying for passage on the largely uncontrolled streets.

needs nourishment. Their commitment to agriculture says *I haven't given up; I'm investing in the future*. These touching rural scenes of Americans and Vietnamese working together to ensure that life goes on are a reminder that acceptance is the last hurdle faced by the grieving.

This is what acceptance looks like to an artist. It looks like the normal bustle of the city. Plans for a meal. Commitment to the status quo (even when the status quo involves killing your enemy). Hanging

81. *Progress in the Highlands.*

This is an image related to a United States-led effort to diversify Vietnam's agriculture by plowing fields in the highlands for planting potatoes, which, it was thought, could be an alternative to the rice that had been grown for many years. The rainy season made it very difficult to plow, and the image features skeptical Vietnamese watching the initiation of the unsuccessful efforts.

82. *Stuck in the Highlands.*

During the attempts to plow fields for the planting of potatoes, one of the Vietnamese involved in the project drove the tractor—a John Deere that I remember was brought over to Vietnam especially for the efforts—and got it stuck in the muddy, monsoon-soaked field. The amusement of those standing by as attempts are made to extricate the equipment is apparent.

83. *Commuting Back to the Village.*

This drawing shows the return back to Gia Vuc village after the fruitless and challenging exercise of attempting to plow fields in the outlying hills for planting potatoes. The attempts were made a few kilometers outside of Gia Vuc, and those present were exposed to potential enemy fire, but were not attacked. The driver was the Green Beret medic, Sergeant Norman Bircher, who was later wounded.

out in a thatch-hut jungle neighborhood. Fighting congestion and chaos on land and sea. Or maybe just trying to grow potatoes. Acceptance is not a "something." It's a process—a mind-set that gets applied repeatedly to conditions and events that remain in constant flux. Acceptance signals a return to normal, a restoration of balance, an infusion into the soul of all the vital nutrients that have been missing. Maybe that's why *Supplies* sums up Gene's view of acceptance so well: *acceptance is the ship that restocks our inner warehouse after it's been depleted by denial, anger, depression, and all the other things that grief forces us to handle.*

84. *Supplies.*

The heaviest materials and equipment needed in Vietnam, such as the Jeep in the foreground, were transported on ships, one of which is seen here being unloaded by Vietnamese for the U.S. base in Da Nang.

85. *I've Got Rhythm.*

This image of a Vietnamese woman carrying a balanced but heavy load was published in October 1965, under the title *The Vietnam Shuffle.* Da Nang was a much more provincial city than cosmopolitan Saigon, of significant size but not nearly so modern. It was more common there to see people carrying things using this balancing device than in the larger city.

But that's not Gene's final message. He leaves us with something just as truthful, but more emotionally impactful. Something that definitively sums things up. Gene assigns this task to *I've Got Rhythm.* A peasant woman, carrying a heavy load in her belly, as well as on her back. She's walking toward the future.

Game over. Acceptance. Kübler-Ross wins again.

Epilogue
Welcome Home

We are so privileged to be a part of this and just wanted you to
know . . . that we will never forget them.
—Paul Revere[1]

Eventually the grieving process ends. Grief resolves. The world
improves. Whatever your problem is, you "get over it."

Or at least that's the way it's supposed to work. Except that
sometimes it doesn't. Maybe you never stop denying that something
terrible has happened. Maybe you stay angry. Or depressed. Maybe
acceptance is, in some cases, an unachievable outcome.

Or maybe your grief eventually resolves, but not without leaving
behind painful, ugly scars and open, festering wounds.

Most combatants serve their time, return home, and reassim-
ilate into society. The war gradually disappears into the past (as
should most adverse things experienced in youth) and the future
moves in and takes over. But for some, the legacy of the Vietnam War is one of unresolved grief, alienation, perpetual anger,
intractable fear, alcoholism, drugs, crime, and other predictable
consequences. Damaged returnees, relatively small in number but
nonetheless large in human significance, continue to pose a nasty
reminder of the high cost of war, quietly gnawing at the conscience
of those of us who stayed home in safety and comfort. Who can forget that many of these soldiers returned home without the thanks,
welcome, or the respect they deserved—survivors who resolved the
direct grief imposed by war only to face new, unexpected sources
of grief at home.

Maybe it's too late to say thank-you and welcome them home.
Or maybe it's not?

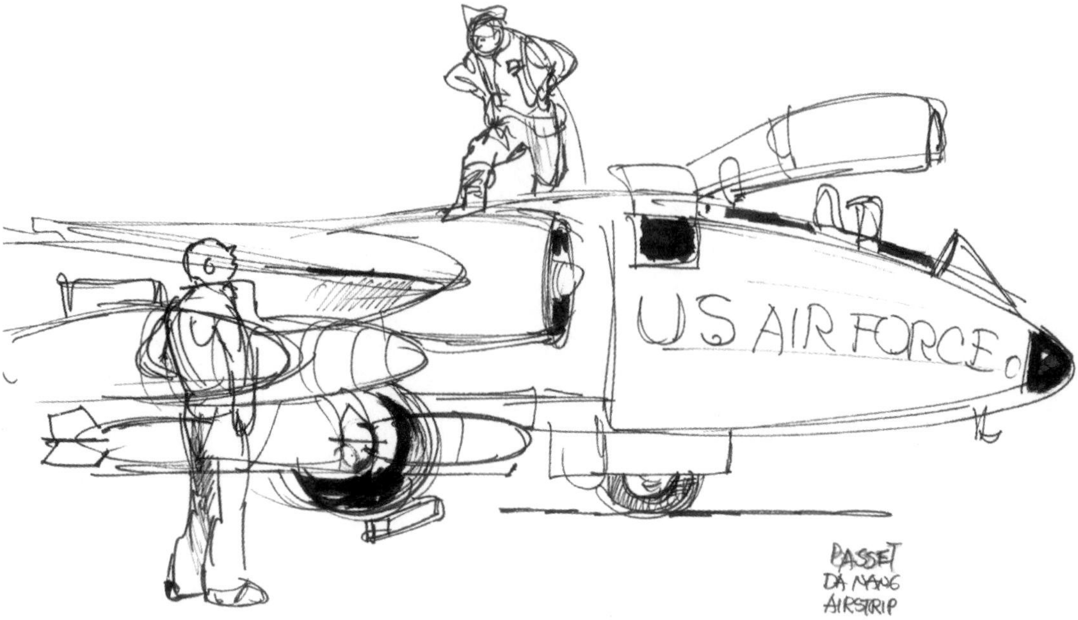
US AIR FORCE
BASSET
DA NANG
AIRSTRIP

86. *Welcome Home.*

Notes

Bibliography

Notes

Preface

1. http://www.goodreads.com/shelf/show/vietnam-war?page=7.

2. A few must-sees for serious war movie fans include Cimino's *The Deer Hunter* (1978), Coppola's epic *Apocalypse Now* (1979), Kubrick's *Full Metal Jacket* (1987), and Oliver Stone's ambitious trilogy: *Platoon* (1986), *Born on the Fourth of July* (1989), and *Heaven and Earth* (1993). For those who like a few laughs with their war stories, Robin Williams is worth catching in *Good Morning, Vietnam*. And for big fans of "the Duke," there's John Wayne's *The Green Berets* (1968).

3. http://www.english.illinois.edu/maps/vietnam/timeline.htm.

4. http://www.veteranshour.com/vietnam_war_statistics.htm.

5. Speech at Tulane University, April 23, 1975. In *Gerald R. Ford*, ed. Douglas Brinkley (New York: Times Books, 2007), 89–98.

6. Jorge Lewinski, *The Camera at War: A History of War Photography from 1848 to the Present Day* (New York: Book Sales, 1987); Susan D. Moeller, *Shooting War: Photography and the American Experience of Combat* (New York: Basic Books, 1989).

7. Elisabeth Kübler-Ross, *On Death and Dying* (New York: Macmillan, 1969).

8. Russell Friedman and John W. James, "The Myth of the Stages of Loss, Death and Grief," *Skeptic Magazine* 14, no. 2 (2012).

9. Weng Marc Lim, "Revisiting Kübler-Ross's Five Stages of Grief: Some Comments on the iPhone 5," *Journal of Social Sciences* 9 (2013): 11–13.

10. Elisabeth Kübler-Ross and David Kessler, *On Grief and Grieving: Finding the Meaning of Grief Through the Five Stages of Loss* (New York: Scribner, 2005).

11. Meghan O'Rourke, "Good Grief: Is There a Better Way to Be Bereaved?" *New Yorker*, February 1, 2010, http://www.newyorker.com/arts/critics/atlarge/20 10/02/01/100201crat_atlarge_orourke?currentPage=all.

1. Denial

1. Wilfried Ver Eecke, "The Complex Phenomenon of Denial," in *Denial, Negation, and the Forces of the Negative: Freud, Hegel, Lacan, Spitz, and Sophocles* (Albany: State University of New York Press, 2006).

2. John McCrone, *The Myth of Irrationality: The Science of the Mind from Plato to Star Trek* (New York: Carroll & Graf, 1994).

3. P. Salander and G. Windahl, "Does 'Denial' Really Cover Our Everyday Experiences in Clinical Oncology? A Critical View from a Psychoanalytic Perspective on the Use of 'Denial,'" *British Journal of Medical Psychology* 72 (1999): 267–79.

4. M. Murray and L. Neilson, "Denial: Coping or cop-out?" *Canadian Nurse* 90 (1994):33–35.

5. M. S. Vos, H. Putter, H. C. van Houwelingen, and H. C. de Haes, "Denial in Lung Cancer Patients: A Longitudinal Study," *Psycho-oncology* 17 (2008):1163–71.

6. T. Rabinowitz and R. Peirson, "'Nothing Is Wrong, Doctor': Understanding and Managing Denial in Patients with Cancer," *Cancer Invest* 24 (2006):68–76.

7. There's an old joke in psychiatry that helps students to remember the difference between someone who is psychotic and someone who's neurotic. "A psychotic patient thinks that two plus two equals five. A neurotic patient knows damn well that two plus two equals four—he just can't stand the thought of it."

8. Michael McKusick, M.D., e-mail communication to author, January 12, 2011.

9. http://www.mayoclinic.org/healthy-living/adult-health/indepth/denial/art -20047926.

10. Although neither of these two drawings are meant to imply that anyone depicted in them feels "not responsible for [fill in this space with any act you choose] because they were intoxicated at the time," the inclusion of alcohol and smokes in the scenes is a reminder that a rationale for denial can be just a few drinks or smokes away. I'm not implying that something more than tobacco is present here. As Freud (once again, allegedly) noted, "Sometimes a cigar IS just a cigar." Alan C. Elms, "Apocryphal Freud: Sigmund Freud's Most Famous 'Quotations' and Their Actual Sources," in *Sigmund Freud and His Impact on the Modern World: The Annual of Psychoanalysis,* ed. Jerome A. Winer and James William Anderson. (Hillsdale, NJ: Analytic Press, 2001), 83–104.

11. http://www.youtube.com/watch?v=PgqhaZmPFRg.

2. Anger

1. *Aggressive Driving: Research Update* (Washington, DC: AAA Foundation for Traffic Safety, April 2009).

2. http://www.psychologytoday.com/blog/evil-deeds/200904/anger-disorder -what-it-is-and-what-we-can-do-about-it.

3. http://www.sott.net/article/152028-Whats-the-true-cause-of-anger.

4. R. G. Smart, M. Asbridge, R. E. Mann, and E. M. Adlaf, "Psychiatric Distress among Road Rage Victims and Perpetrators," *Canadian Journal of Psychiatry* 48 (2003):681–88; J. L. Deffenbacher, D. M. Deffenbacher, R. S. Lynch, and T. L. Richards, "Anger, Aggression, and Risky Behavior: A Comparison of High and Low Anger Drivers," *Behaviour Research and Therapy* 41, no. 6 (2003): 701–18.

5. Frank Moore Colby, *The Colby Essays*, vol. 2 (New York: Harper and Brothers, 1926), 92.

6. Letter to James E. Yeatman, May 21, 1865. In *Sherman and His Campaigns*, ed. Samuel M. Bowman and Richard B. Irwin (New York: Vivisphere Publishing, 2000).

7. Gene, a true Yankee fan, claims it's "no contest as to which team is better." We'll make him stick to drawing. According to *Wikipedia*, as of July 4, 2011, there have been 2,091 regular-season games between the teams, with an all-time record (favoring the Yankees) of 1,140-955-14. By my calculations, the Yankees are just barely above .500 in this series (.544). That's too close to call. http://wiki.answers .com/Q/What_is_the_New_York_Yankees_vs_Boston_Red_Sox_all-time_record.

8. Lester C. Olson, Carla A. Finnegan, and Diane S. Hope, *Visual Rhetoric: A Reader in Communication and American Culture* (New York: Sage Publications, 2008), 178.

9. Jarmel Bell, *The Quote: Character Education Manual* (Bloomington: Authorhouse, 2011), 52.

3. Bargaining

1. http://www.pbs.org/wgbh/commandingheights/shared/minitext/int_milton friedman.html.

2. Chester Louis Karrass, *"In Business as in Life—You Don't Get What You Deserve, You Get What You Negotiate"* (Beverly Hills: Stanford Street Press, 1996).

4. Depression

1. Mark Twain, http://www.goodreads.com/quotes/257244-humor-is-tragedy -plus-time.

2. William Ernest Henley, *A Book of Verses* (New York: Charles Scribner's Sons, 1893).

3. Richard Stumpf, In *Catastrophe 1914: Europe Goes to War*, by Max Hastings (New York: Random House, 2013).

5. Acceptance

1. W. T. O'Donohue and J. E. Fisher, eds., *General Principles and Empirically Supported Techniques of Cognitive Behavior Therapy* (Hoboken, NJ: John Wiley & Sons, 2009).

Epilogue

1. With support from his band, the Raiders, Paul Revere comments on his long-standing participation with Ride to the Wall, a nonprofit foundation that he helped establish to bring attention and support to veterans. His desire was to "give Vietnam War veterans the 'welcome home' they never got—but deserve."

Bibliography

AAA Foundation for Traffic Safety. *Aggressive Driving: Research Update.* April 2009.

Attardo, Salvatore, ed. *Encyclopedia of Humor Studies.* New York: Sage Books, 2014.

Bell, Jarmel. *The Quote: Character Education Manual.* Bloomington: Authorhouse, 2011.

Bowman, Samuel M., and Richard B. Irwin. *Sherman and His Campaigns: A Military Biography.* New York: CB Richardson, 1865.

Brinkley, Douglas. *Gerald R. Ford.* New York: Times Books, 2007.

Colby, Frank Moore. *The Colby Essays*, vol. 2. New York: Harper and Brothers, 1926.

"Commanding Heights: Milton Friedman." PBS. http://www.pbs.org /wgbh/commandingheights/shared/minitext/int_miltonfriedman.html.

Deffenbacher J. L., et al. "Anger, Aggression, and Risky Behavior: A Comparison of High and Low Anger Drivers." *Behaviour Research Therapy* 41, no. 6 (2003): 701–18.

Diamond, Stephen A. "Anger Disorder: What It Is and What We Can Do about It." *Psychology Today*, April 20, 2009. http://www.psychology today.com/blog/evil-deeds/200904/anger-disorder-what-it-is-and-what -we-can-do-about-it.

Elms, Alan C. "Apocryphal Freud: Sigmund Freud's Most Famous 'Quotations' and Their Actual Sources." In *Sigmund Freud and His Impact on the Modern World: The Annual of Psychoanalysis*, edited by Jerome A. Winer and James William Anderson, 83–104. Hillsdale, NJ: Analytic Press, 2001.

Friedman, Russell, and John W. James. "The Myth of the Stages of Loss, Death and Grief," *Skeptic Magazine*, 2012.

Henley, William Ernest. *A Book of Verses.* New York: Charles Scribner's Sons, 1893.

Karrass, Chester Louis. *"In Business as in Life—You Don't Get What You Deserve, You Get What You Negotiate."* Beverly Hills: Stanford Street Press, 1996.

Kübler-Ross, Elisabeth. *On Death and Dying.* New York: Macmillan, 1969.

Kübler-Ross, Elisabeth, and David Kessler. *On Grief and Grieving: Finding the Meaning of Grief Through the Five Stages of Loss.* New York: Scribner, 2005.

Lewinski, Jorge. *The Camera at War: A History of War Photography from 1848 to the Present Day.* New York: Book Sales, 1987.

Lim, Weng Marc. "Revisiting Kübler-Ross's Five Stages of Grief: Some Comments on the iPhone 5," *Journal of Social Sciences* 9 (2013):11–13.

Mayo Clinic Staff. "Denial: When It Helps, When It Hurts." Mayo Clinic, May 20, 2014. http://www.mayoclinic.org/healthy-living/adult-health /in-depth/denial/art-20047926.

McCrone, John. *The Myth of Irrationality: The Science of the Mind from Plato to Star Trek.* New York: Carroll & Graf Publishers, 1994.

McKusick, Michael, M.D. E-mail communication to author, January 12, 2011.

Moeller, Susan D. *Shooting War: Photography and the American Experience of Combat.* New York: Basic Books, 1989.

Murray, Mary Ann, and Lee Neilson. "Denial: Coping or Cop-out?" *Canadian Nurses' Association* 90 (1994): 33–35.

O'Donohue, William T., and Jane E. Fisher, eds. *General Principles and Empirically Supported Techniques of Cognitive Behavior Therapy.* Hoboken, NJ: John Wiley & Sons, 2009.

Olson, Lester C., Carla A. Finnegan, and Diane S. Hope. *Visual Rhetoric: A Reader in Communication and American Culture.* New York: Sage Publications, 2008.

O'Rourke, Meghan. "Good Grief: Is There a Better Way to Be Bereaved?" *New Yorker*, February 1, 2010. http://www.newyorker.com/arts/critics /atlarge/2010/02/01/100201crat_atlarge_orourke?currentPage=all.

Rabinowitz, Terry, and Ryan Patrick Peirson. "'Nothing Is Wrong, Doctor': Understanding and Managing Denial in Patients with Cancer." *Cancer Investigation* 24 (2006): 68–76.

Salander, Par, and Gunnar Windahl. "Does 'Denial' Really Cover Our Everyday Experiences in Clinical Oncology? A Critical View from a Psychoanalytic Perspective on the Use of 'Denial.'" *British Journal of Medical Psychology* 72 (1999): 267–79.

Smart, Reginald G., et al. "Psychiatric Distress among Road Rage Victims and Perpetrators." *Canadian Journal of Psychiatry* 48 (2003): 681–88.

Stumpf, Richard. In *Catastrophe 1914: Europe Goes to War*, by Max Hastings. New York: Random House, 2013.

Ver Eecke, Wilfried. *Denial, Negation, and the Forces of the Negative: Freud, Hegel, Lacan, Spitz, and Sophocles.* Albany: State Univ. of New York Press, 2006.

"Vietnam War Timeline." Modern American Poetry. http://www.english .illinois.edu/maps/vietnam/timeline.htm.

Vos, Martina S., et al. "Denial in Lung Cancer Patients: A Longitudinal Study." *Psycho-oncology* 17 (2008): 1163–71.

Thom Rooke is a Professor of Medicine at the Mayo Clinic in Rochester, Minnesota. He holds an endowed chair in vascular medicine, and is former head of the section of vascular medicine and director of the Gonda Vascular Center. Raised in Detroit, Michigan, Dr. Rooke received his Bachelor of Science at the University of Michigan, and M.D. degree at Johns Hopkins University in Baltimore, Maryland. He did his residency in internal medicine and subspecialty training in cardiovascular diseases at Mayo Clinic; he is a board certified cardiologist and vascular medicine specialist. The author of scores of scientific articles, medical books, editorials, and essays, Dr. Rooke is an internationally renowned expert in cardiovascular disease. He is a sought-after lecturer in his areas of scientific expertise, and is known for his creative, lively, and entertaining talks. Dr. Rooke lives in Rochester with his wife, Julie, and their three sons.